Mathematics

Math Diagnosis and Intervention System

Booklet M
Problem Solving
in Grades 4–6

Overview of Math Diagnosis and Intervention System

The system can be used in a variety of situations:

- **During school** Use the system for intervention on prerequisite skills at the beginning of the year, the beginning of a chapter, or the beginning of a lesson. Use for intervention during the chapter when more is needed beyond the resources already provided for the lesson.
- **After-school, Saturday-school, summer-school (intersession) programs** Use the system for intervention offered in special programs. The booklets are also available as workbooks.

The system provides resources for:

- **Assessment** For each of Grades K–6, a Diagnostic Test is provided that assesses that grade. Use a test at the start of the year for entry-level assessment or anytime during the year as a summative evaluation.
- **Diagnosis** An item analysis identifies areas where intervention is needed.
- **Intervention** Booklets A–M identify specific topics and assign a number to each topic, for example, A12 or E10. For each topic, there is a page of Intervention Practice and a two-page Intervention Lesson that cover the same content taught in a lesson of the program.
- **Monitoring** The Teaching Guide provides both Individual Record Forms and Class Record Forms to monitor student progress.

PEARSON
Scott Foresman

Editorial Offices: Glenview, Illinois • Parsippany, New Jersey • New York, New York

Sales Offices: Needham, Massachusetts • Duluth, Georgia • Glenview, Illinois
Coppell, Texas • Ontario, California • Mesa, Arizona

ISBN: 0-328-07656-2

Copyright © Pearson Education, Inc.
All Rights Reserved. Printed in the United States of America. This publication or parts thereof, may be used with appropriate equipment to reproduce copies for classroom use only.

4 5 6 7 8 9 10 V084 12 11 10 09 08 07 06 05

Table of Contents

		Intervention Lesson Pages	Intervention Practice Pages	\multicolumn{4}{l}{The same content is taught in the Scott Foresman-Addison Wesley Mathematics Program}
				Gr. 3	Gr. 4	Gr. 5	Gr. 6
Booklet M							
Problem Solving Skills							
M1	Problem Solving Skill: Choose an Operation	1	93	6-11	5-11		
M2	Problem Solving Skill: Choose an Operation	3	94			8-15	8-4
M3	Problem Solving Skill: Multiple-Step Problems	5	95	5-8	3-11		
M4	Problem Solving Skill: Multiple-Step Problems	7	96			4-8	3-12
M5	Problem Solving Skill: Extra or Missing Information	9	97	9-16	12-4		
M6	Problem Solving Skill: Extra or Missing Information	11	98			7-6	11-13
M7	Problem Solving Skill: Exact or Estimate	13	99	3-11	10-12		
M8	Problem Solving Skill: Exact or Estimate	15	100			10-10	4-8
M9	Problem Solving Skill: Read and Understand	17	101	1-6	1-4		
M10	Problem Solving Skill: Read and Understand	19	102			1-6	1-7
M11	Problem Solving Skill: Plan and Solve	21	103	1-11	1-8		
M12	Problem Solving Skill: Plan and Solve	23	104			1-10	1-12
M13	Problem Solving Skill: Look Back and Check	25	105	1-14	1-13		
M14	Problem Solving Skill: Look Back and Check	27	106			1-14	1-16
M15	Problem Solving Skill: Translating Words to Expressions	29	107	7-13	2-10		
M16	Problem Solving Skill: Translating Words to Expressions	31	108			2-13	12-4
M17	Problem Solving Skill: Writing to Explain	33	109	2-12	12-10		
M18	Problem Solving Skill: Writing to Explain	35	110			9-15, 12-8	5-10, 6-8
M19	Problem Solving Skill: Writing to Compare	37	111	4-8	4-4		
M20	Problem Solving Skill: Writing to Compare	39	112			5-9	9-12
M21	Problem Solving Skill: Writing to Describe	41	113	8-14, 10-8	8-9, 11-13		
M22	Problem Solving Skill: Writing to Describe	43	114			6-8	11-16
M23	Problem Solving Skill: Interpreting Remainders	45	115	11-15	7-6		
M24	Problem Solving Skill: Interpreting Remainders	47	116		3-12	2-8	

iii

Table of Contents continued

		Intervention Lesson Pages	Intervention Practice Pages	The same content is taught in the Scott Foresman-Addison Wesley Mathematics Program			
Booklet M				Gr. 3	Gr. 4	Gr. 5	Gr. 6
Problem Solving Strategies						
M25	Problem Solving Strategy: Draw a Picture	49	117	3-5	9-5		
M26	Problem Solving Strategy: Draw a Picture	51	118			9-11	9-5
M27	Problem Solving Strategy: Make an Organized List	53	119	10-5	6-4		
M28	Problem Solving Strategy: Make an Organized List	55	120			2-6	5-5
M29	Problem Solving Strategy: Make a Table	57	121	5-4	3-5		
M30	Problem Solving Strategy: Make a Table	59	122			11-5	3-5
M31	Problem Solving Strategy: Make a Graph	61	123	4-14	4-11		
M32	Problem Solving Strategy: Make a Graph	63	124			5-5	11-8
M33	Problem Solving Strategy: Use Objects	65	125			10-4	6-4
M34	Problem Solving Strategy: Use Objects	67	126	8-3	8-12		
M35	Problem Solving Strategy: Look for a Pattern	69	127	6-6	2-9		
M36	Problem Solving Strategy: Look for a Pattern	71	128			3-4	4-3
M37	Problem Solving Strategy: Try, Test, and Revise	73	129	7-4	5-7		
M38	Problem Solving Strategy: Try, Test, and Revise	75	130			4-3	12-3
M39	Problem Solving Strategy: Write a Number Sentence	77	131	2-4	7-10		
M40	Problem Solving Strategy: Write a Number Sentence	79	132			12-4	2-13
M41	Problem Solving Strategy: Use Logical Reasoning	81	133	11-11	10-6		
M42	Problem Solving Strategy: Use Logical Reasoning	83	134			7-15	10-6
M43	Problem Solving Strategy: Solve a Simpler Problem	85	135	9-11	11-8		
M44	Problem Solving Strategy: Solve a Simpler Problem	87	136			6-7	7-7
M45	Problem Solving Strategy: Work Backward	89	137	12-3	12-9		
M46	Problem Solving Strategy: Work Backward	91	138			8-9	8-10

Name _____

Intervention Lesson **M1**

Math Diagnosis and Intervention System

Problem-Solving Skill: Choose an Operation

Read and Understand

Marla made 5 batches of muffins. There were 6 muffins in each batch. How many muffins did Marla make in all?

You can draw a picture to show the main idea.

⑥ ⑥ ⑥ ⑥ ⑥

Plan and Solve

The picture can also help you decide whether to add, subtract, or multiply.

You are putting together equal groups, so you should multiply.

$5 \times 6 = 30$

Marla made 30 muffins in all.

Look Back and Check

Because each batch has the same number, multiplication is the best operation to find the total.

Draw a picture to show the main idea. Use the picture to help write a number sentence and solve the problem.

1. Joan earns $5 an hour mowing lawns. She earns $3 an hour raking leaves. How much will Joan make if she mows lawns for 4 hours?

   _____

2. Carla has 16 marbles and 15 stickers. Ten of Carla's marbles are red. The rest are blue. How many blue marbles does Carla have?

   _____

1

Name _____

Intervention Lesson **M1**

Math Diagnosis and Intervention System

Problem-Solving Skill: Choose an Operation (continued)

Draw a picture or write a number sentence to show the main idea. Then use the picture to write a number sentence and solve the problem.

Use the data in the table for Questions 3 and 4.

| Number of CDs Sold ||
Day	Number Sold
Thursday	6
Friday	8
Saturday	15
Sunday	11
Monday	10

3. Were more CDs sold on Thursday and Friday together, or on Saturday?

   _____

4. Two times as many CDs were sold on Tuesday as on Monday. How many CDs were sold on Tuesday?

   _____

5. Lakesha counted 20 cars that passed her house. Exactly 12 cars were white, and the rest were red. How many red cars passed Lakesha's house? _____

6. **Writing in Math** Explain how you solved Question 5. Tell what operation you used.

   _____

   _____

Test Prep Circle the correct letter for the answer.

7. Bill has 17 baseball cards and 19 basketball cards. Which operation must you use to find the total number of cards?

   A addition   **C** multiplication
   B subtraction   **D** division

8. Connie feeds her dog 3 pounds of food a week. How many pounds of food does she use to feed her dog for 6 weeks?

   A 9 pounds   **C** 18 pounds
   B 12 pounds   **D** 24 pounds

Name _____

Math Diagnosis and Intervention System

Intervention Lesson **M2**

Problem-Solving Skill: Choose an Operation

Read and Understand

Ms. Kim's fifth-grade class took a survey of favorite amusement park rides. How many students DIDN'T choose the Magnum ride?

12 students chose the Magnum ride. The rest didn't choose the Magnum.

Ride	Number of Students
Cork Screw	4
Gemini	7
Magnum	12
Mine Ride	4
Water Ride	3

Plan and Solve

Choose an operation:

1. **Add** to find the total number of students $4 + 7 + 12 + 4 + 3 = 30$

2. **Subtract** to find the difference: $30 - 12 = 18$.

So, 18 students didn't choose the Magnum as their favorite ride.

Look Back and Check

$18 + 12 = 30$. The answer checks.

Choose an operation. Then solve the problem.

1. How many students liked the Gemini and Magnum? _____

2. A 12-quart bucket contains $6\frac{1}{2}$ quarts of water. How much more water can be added to the bucket?

_____

3

Problem-Solving Skill: Choose an Operation (continued)

Choose an operation and solve the problem.

3. Mollie biked 3 miles to the library, another mile to the grocery store, and 2 miles home. What was the total distance that she biked?

4. A large can of fruit weighs $18\frac{1}{2}$ ounces. Without the juice, the fruit weighs $15\frac{1}{2}$ ounces. What is the weight of the juice?

5. **Writing in Math** Write and solve a story problem to match the picture.

18	
12	d

Test Prep Circle the correct letter for the answer.

6. A restaurant needs 48 pounds of noodles for lasagna. Each package contains 8 pounds. How many packages of lasagna noodles will be needed?

    A 56　　　　**B** 40　　　　**C** 8　　　　**D** 6

7. Which operation will you use to solve the problem? Ms. Eduardo's punch bowl holds $9\frac{1}{4}$ quarts of punch when it is completely filled. It now contains $2\frac{1}{2}$ quarts of punch. How much more punch must be added to fill the bowl?

    A add　　　　**B** subtract　　　　**C** multiply　　　　**D** divide

Name _____

Intervention Lesson **M3**

Math Diagnosis and Intervention System

Problem-Solving Skill: Multiple-Step Problems

To solve some problems, you need to answer hidden questions.

At the sports store, Hannah bought 2 baseballs, and Jim bought 3 baseballs. The baseballs cost $6 each. How much did they spend?

Read and Understand

Find how much Hannah and Jim spent altogether.

First, answer the hidden question:

How many baseballs did Hannah and Jim buy altogether? $2 + 3 = 5$

Then, solve the problem:

Number of baseballs Hannah and Jim bought	×	Price of a baseball	=	Amount Hannah and Jim spent altogether
5	×	$6	=	$30

Hannah and Jim spent $30 altogether.

Write the hidden question.

1. It costs $3 to rent a video. Sue rented 4 videos, and Fran rented 3 videos. How much did they pay in all?

   _____

   _____

2. There are 5 blank video tapes in a pack. Jamal bought 2 packs, and Bob bought 1 pack. How many blank video tapes did they buy in all?

   _____

   _____

5

Name _____

Intervention Lesson **M3**

Problem-Solving Skill: Multiple-Step Problems (continued)

Write and answer the hidden question. Then solve the problem.

Use the graph to answer Questions 3–5.

Favorite Snack	
Fruit	☺ ☺ ☺
Sandwiches	☺ ☺
Cheese	☺
Pretzels	☺ ☺ ☺ ☺

Each ☺ = 3 votes.

3. How many students voted for fruit or cheese?

   _____

   _____

   _____

4. How many more students voted for pretzels than voted for sandwiches?

   _____

   _____

   _____

5. **Number Sense** If ☺ = 5 votes, how many students voted for pretzels?

   _____

Test Prep Circle the correct letter for the answer.

6. There are 4 boxes of orange juice in a pack. There are 5 boxes of grape juice in a pack. What hidden question can you use to find how many boxes there are in 2 orange packs and 3 grape packs?

   A How many of each kind of juice box are there?

   B How many boxes of orange juice are in a pack?

   C How much does each pack cost?

   D How many more boxes of grape juice than orange juice are there?

7. Movie tickets cost $5 for adults and $2 for children under the age of 12. How much will it cost for 3 adults and 2 children to go to the movies?

   A $4   **B** $10   **C** $19   **D** $35

Name _____

Intervention Lesson **M4**

Problem-Solving Skill
Multiple-Step Problems

Example

Carmen bought 2 DVDs on sale for $21.99 each. She gave the clerk a $3 discount coupon and a $50 bill. The tax was $2.64. How much change should she receive?

Read and Understand

Identify key facts and details. What is the problem asking?
2 DVDs were bought for $21.99 each. The tax was $2.64.
A $3 discount coupon was given. Carmen gave the clerk $50.
What was her change?

Plan and Solve

What hidden questions are in the problem?
Hidden Question 1: How much did the two DVDs cost with tax?
$21.99 × 2 = $43.98 and $43.98 + $2.64 = $46.62

Hidden Question 2: What was the cost with the coupon?
$46.62 − $3.00 = $43.62

Answer: What was her change?
$50.00 − $43.62 = $6.38
Carmen received $6.38 in change.

Write and answer the hidden questions. Then solve the problem. Use the table.

1. Two families went bowling. They paid for 4 adult games and 4 bumper bowling games, but no one rented shoes. What was the total cost they paid?

Bowling Prices (per game)	
Adults	$3.35
Bumper bowling	$3.70
Shoe rental (per person)	$2.00

_____

_____

_____

7

Name _____

Intervention Lesson **M4**

Problem-Solving Skill: Multiple-Step Problems (continued)

Write and answer the hidden questions. Then solve the problem. Use the table for Questions 2, 3, and 4.

Amusement Park Tickets	
Adults	$42.00
Junior tickets (under 48 in.)	$27.00
Starlight (after 5 P.M.)	$32.00

2. The Kim family bought 3 adult tickets and 2 junior tickets. What was the total cost of the tickets?

_____
_____
_____

3. The Bondi family purchased 4 Starlight tickets for the amusement park. How much money did they save by buying 4 Starlight tickets rather than 4 adult tickets?

_____
_____
_____

4. **Number Sense** Could you have subtracted the Starlight ticket price from the adult ticket price and multiplied by 4 to get the total savings by the Bondi family in Question 3?

_____
_____

Test Prep Circle the correct letter for the answer.

5. Ms. Garza purchased 20 copies of the same activity book. The cost, including the tax of $3.72, was $48.72. What was the cost of one activity book?

   A $2.44   B $2.32   C $2.25   D $2.20

6. A customer rents 3 DVDs and 2 games. Each DVD rental is $4, and each game rental is $2. The customer pays with two $10 bills. How much change does the customer receive?

   A $16.00   B $4.00   C $2.00   D $1.50

8

Name _____

Intervention Lesson **M5**

Problem-Solving Skill
Extra or Missing Information

Example

Sally's painting is 14 inches long and 12 inches wide. Julie's painting is 16 inches long. How much longer is Julie's painting than Sally's painting?

Read and Understand

What do you know?
Sally's painting is 14 inches long. Sally's painting is 12 inches wide. Julie's painting is 16 inches long.

What do you need to find?
I need to find how much longer one painting is than the other.

Is there any extra or missing information?
Yes, I don't need to know how wide Sally's painting is.

Plan and Solve

To find the difference between the lengths, I need to subtract.
16 − 14 = 2

Julie's painting is 2 inches longer than Sally's painting.

Write the extra or missing information. Solve the problem if enough information is given.

1. Jason bought a red sweater and a black sweater. His change was $5. How much did Jason pay for both sweaters?

   _____

   _____

9

Name _____

Intervention Lesson **M5**

Problem-Solving Skill: Extra or Missing Information (continued)

Write the extra or missing information. Solve the problem if enough information is given.

Use the graph for Questions 2–3.

2. Turtles received 4 fewer votes than cats and 2 more votes than rabbits. How many votes did turtles receive?

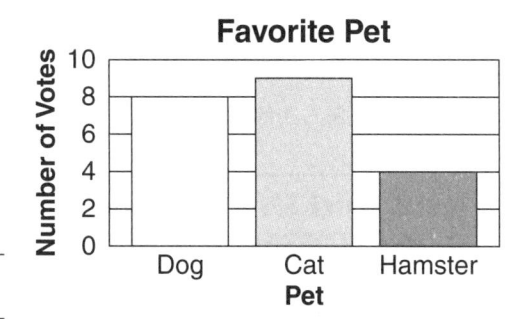

   _____

   _____

Favorite Pet

(Bar graph: Dog = 8, Cat = 9, Hamster = 4; Number of Votes on y-axis, Pet on x-axis)

3. How many more students voted for dogs than horses?

   _____

   _____

4. **Writing in Math** Rose's painting is 12 inches long. Will it fit in a frame that has length of 12 inches and a width of 8 inches? Explain.

   _____

Test Prep Circle the correct letter for the answer.

5. Bill has 23 baseball cards, 12 basketball cards, and 4 soccer cards. Each card cost $1.00. What extra information is not needed to find how many cards Bill has in all?

   A Bill has 23 baseball cards.
   B Bill has 12 basketball cards.
   C Bill has 4 soccer cards.
   D Each card cost $1.00.

6. Harold placed 3 pieces of string end-to-end on his desk. The first piece is 16 inches long and the second is 8 inches long. What information do you need to find the total length of the 3 pieces of string?

   A the length of the first piece
   B the length of the third piece
   C the length of the second piece
   D the length of Harold's desk

Name _____

Intervention Lesson **M6**

Problem-Solving Skill
Extra or Missing Information

Example

Nick bought 2 copies of the same book for a total of $10.80. The length of each book was 8 inches. The combined weight of the 2 books is 1.6 pounds. How much did each book cost?

Read and Understand

What do you know? Nick bought 2 books.
Identify key facts The total cost of the books is $10.80.
Each book is 8 inches long and weighs 1.6 pounds.
What are you trying to find? How much does each book cost?

Plan and Solve

Ask yourself: Is there enough information to solve the problem?

2 books cost $10.80. What does one book cost?
$10.80 ÷ 2 = $5.40 for one book

Decide if each problem has extra or missing information. Solve if you have enough information.

1. Ms. Johns buys a pair of ducks. She gives the clerk $40 and receives $15 change. She has decided to name the ducks George and Freida. Each duck cost the same amount.

    a. How much does each duck cost? _____

    b. What extra information is given? _____

2. Mikel charges $45 per hour for computer repairs. He repaired 4 computers on Tuesday. How much money did Mikel earn?

    _____

11

Name _____

Intervention Lesson **M6**

Problem-Solving Skill: Extra or Missing Information (continued)

Decide if each problem has extra or missing information. Solve if you have enough information.

3. Renee works for 2 hours after school on Monday, Wednesday, and Thursday. She is working to save money for summer camp that costs $175. She earns $6 per hour. How many weeks must Renee work to be sure she has enough money?

   _____

For Questions 4–5, use the table at the right.

4. The Delta Pool keeps monthly pool attendance records. The pool charges $1 for each person over 12 years old and $0.50 for each child aged 5 to 12. How much money did the pool make in June?

Pool Attendance	
June	1,825
July	2,472
August	2,217

   _____

   _____

5. The directors want to know how many people used the pool during the 3 months it was open. What was the total attendance? _____

6. **Writing in Math** Write a word problem with too much information.

   _____

   _____

Test Prep Circle the correct letter for the answer.

7. On June 4, Lyle's mom told him that his grandmother would return from vacation in 25 days. On what day did Lyle see his grandmother?

   A June 25   **B** July 4   **C** June 29   **D** not enough information

12

Name _____

Intervention Lesson **M7**

Problem-Solving Skill: Exact or Estimate?

Example

Class 1 collected 295 cans. Class 2 collected 123 cans. Class 3 collected 205 cans. Did the classes collect at least 500 cans?

Read and Understand

Tell what you are trying to find: Did the classes collect at least 500 cans?

Decide if an estimate is enough. Yes, you can compare an estimate to 500 cans.

Plan and Solve

Make an organized list.

295 is about 300.
123 is about 100.
215 is about 200.

Add $300 + 100 + 200 = 600$
Compare   600 is greater than 500.

The students collected more than 500 cans.

For Questions 1–3, use the Sticker problem.

Stickers Tina had 282 stickers. She bought 218 more, and then she got 125 stickers for her birthday. Pat has 875 stickers. Who has more stickers?

1. What do you know, and what are you trying to find?

   _____

   _____

2. Is an estimate enough?

   _____

3. Solve the problem.

   _____

13

Name _____

Intervention Lesson **M7**

Problem-Solving Skill: Exact or Estimate? (continued)

For Questions 4–6, use the Soccer Game problem.

4. What do you know, and what are you trying to find?

> An indoor arena seats 920 people to watch a soccer game. So far, 794 people are seated to watch the soccer game. Can 115 more people be seated in the arena? Explain.

_____

_____

_____

_____

5. Is an estimate enough?

_____

_____

6. Solve the problem. Give your answer in a complete sentence.

_____

_____

Test Prep Circle the correct letter for the answer.

7. Which question can you answer by estimating? Fred has 275 stamps. Marcos has 391 stamps.

   A How many stamps do they have in all?

   B How many more stamps than Fred does Marcos have?

   C Do they have at least 800 stamps in all?

   D How many fewer stamps than Marcos does Fred have?

Name _____

Intervention Lesson **M8**

Math Diagnosis and Intervention System

Problem-Solving Skill: Exact or Estimate?

Example

When you solve a problem, you can sometime use an estimate. An estimate is a quick and easy way to get an answer. Sometimes you will need an exact answer. An exact answer will give more precise information.

How many feet of weather stripping will Mr. Barton need to put around a door 3 feet wide and 7 feet tall?

Read and Understand

What do you know? Mr. Barton wants to install weather stripping.

What are you trying to find? How much weather stripping he will need.

Do you need an exact answer or an estimate? An exact answer.

Plan and Solve

Ask yourself, "How do I find perimeter?" Find the distance around the door.

3 + 3 + 7 + 7 = 20

Mr. Barton will need 20 feet of weather stripping.

Tell whether an exact answer or an estimate is needed. Then solve the problem and check to see if your answer is reasonable.

1. James charges Ms. Bigs 10 cents per square foot to mow her lawn for the entire summer. Her lawn is 50 feet long and 40 feet wide. How much should James charge Ms. Bigs? _____

2. Jason wants to buy lunch. A chicken sandwich costs $3.25, a glass of milk costs $1.10, and a cookie costs $0.50. Jason has $5.00. Can he buy one of each item?

_____

15

Name _____

Intervention Lesson **M8**

Problem-Solving Skill: Exact or Estimate? (continued)

Tell whether an exact answer or an estimate is needed. Then solve the problem and check to see if your answer is reasonable.

3. The perimeter of a piece of paper is 24 inches. What lengths and widths of the piece of paper are possible?

   _____

   _____

   _____

4. Carmen has a section of lawn that needs to be reseeded. It measures 18 feet by 75 feet. How many bags of seed will she need if one bag of seed covers 300 square feet? _____

5. How many square feet of roofing paper does Joe need in order to put a new roof on his dog house? The roof has 2 sides, and each side of the roof measures 3 feet by $2\frac{1}{2}$ feet. _____

6. Carlos's mom wants to plant some new shrubs along one side of the driveway. The driveway is 85 feet long. The shrubs must be planted at least 3 feet apart. About how many shrubs will she need? _____

7. Tina has a board 16 feet long. She is going to cut four 3-foot shelves from the board. How much of the board will she have left? _____

8. **Writing in Math** What determines if an answer should be exact or estimated?

   _____

   _____

Test Prep Circle the correct letter for the answer.

9. Mr. Rohrs knows that it takes 7 bricks to cover 1 square foot of surface area. How many bricks will he need to construct the wall shown?

   A 45 bricks **C** 450 bricks

   B 315 bricks **D** 500 bricks

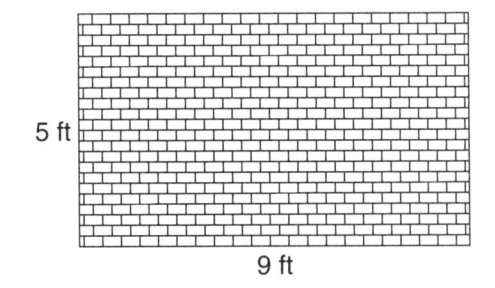

   5 ft, 9 ft

16

Intervention Lesson **M9**

Name _____

Problem-Solving Skill: Read and Understand

Example

Karen had some stickers. She gave 4 butterfly stickers and 5 flag stickers to Bill. How many stickers did Karen give to Bill?

Read and Understand

What do you know? Karen gave Bill 4 butterfly stickers and 5 flag stickers.

What are you trying to find? The total number of stickers Karen gave to Bill.

4 butterfly stickers	5 flag stickers
Total number of stickers	

Plan and Solve

Use addition to find the answer. $4 + 5 = 9$ stickers

Karen gave Bill 9 stickers.

Look Back and Check

Using addition is okay because you need to put together two kinds of stickers.

Solve the problem. Write the answer in a complete sentence.

1. Harold collects stamps. He has 30 stamps from the United States and 20 stamps from other countries. How many more United States stamps does Harold have than foreign stamps?

_____

_____

Name _____

Intervention Lesson **M9**

Math Diagnosis and Intervention System

Problem-Solving Skill: Read and Understand (continued)

Solve each problem. Write the answer in a complete sentence.

2. Some fourth-grade students took a survey about cats and dogs. They found that 7 students like cats the best and 11 students like dogs the best. How many students voted for their favorite pet?

_____
_____

3. Jared ran 2 miles on Monday, 4 miles on Tuesday, and 6 miles on Wednesday. If Jared continued to increase his running by this pattern, how many miles did he run on Thursday?

_____
_____

4. Brittany had 3 pizzas. She cut 1 pizza into 8 slices and 2 pizzas into 6 slices. How many slices of pizza did Brittany have?

_____
_____

5. Writing in Math Explain how you found the answer to Question 4.

_____
_____

Test Prep Circle the correct letter for the answer.

6. Ed counted the fish in his tank. He counted 7 large goldfish and 3 small goldfish. He counted 2 large angelfish and 5 small angelfish. How many large fish are in Ed's tank?

    A 8 large fish   **C** 10 large fish

    B 9 large fish   **D** 17 large fish

Name _____

Intervention Lesson **M10**

Math Diagnosis and Intervention System

Problem-Solving Skill: Read and Understand

Example

Hummingbirds' wings beat about 55 to 75 times per second.
What are the least and greatest numbers of beats *per minute*?

Read and Understand

What do you know?

Identify key details and facts.　　Slowest wing beats are 55 times per second.
　　　　　　　　　　　　　　　　Fastest wing beats are 75 times per second.
　　　　　　　　　　　　　　　　There are 60 seconds in one minute

Plan and Solve

Tell what the question is asking.　　How many beats per minute do their wings
　　　　　　　　　　　　　　　　　beat (greatest and least)?

You multiply beats per second by 60 to get beats per minute.

55 × 60 = 3,300 beats per minute
75 × 60 = 4,500 beats per minute

The least and greatest numbers of beats per minute of hummingbirds'
wings are 3,300 and 4,500.

Use the information to the right.

1. Solve the problem and write your answer in a complete sentence.

_____

_____

_____

_____

> The largest hummingbird in the world weighs about 20 grams. One of the smallest may weigh only 2.2 grams. What is the difference in weight between the smallest and largest hummingbird?

19

Name _____

Intervention Lesson **M10**

Problem-Solving Skill: Read and Understand (continued)

For Questions 2–4, use the information to the right.

> A groundhog lives in a burrow and hibernates during the winter. The length of hibernation varies with the severity of the climate. The groundhog can grow to a length of about 2 ft from nose to the base of the tail. Its bushy tail can be up to about 0.82 ft long. What is the length of a groundhog, including its tail?

2. What do you know?
   a. Tell what you know about the problem in your own words.

   _____
   _____

   b. Identify key facts and details.

   _____
   _____

3. What are you trying to find?

   _____

4. Solve the problem and write your answer in a complete sentence.

   _____
   _____

Test Prep Circle the correct letter for the answer.

Use the information for Questions 5–6.

At the weekend bake sale, the PTA had 2 dozen cakes, 6 dozen cupcakes, 18 dozen brownies, and 14 dozen cookies.

5. How many more brownies were donated than cakes?

   A 18 dozen   **C** 12 dozen

   B 16 dozen   **D** 8 dozen

6. The bake sale committee sold half of the cupcakes and cookies the first day. How many dozen were sold on this day?

   A 20 dozen   **C** 10 dozen

   B 15 dozen   **D** 5 dozen

Name _____

Intervention Lesson **M11**

Math Diagnosis and Intervention System

Problem-Solving Skill: Plan and Solve

Example

You can use these steps to plan and solve a problem.

On Day 1, Ti gets 1 dime. Each day she doubles the number of dimes she gets. How much money will Ti have after 4 days?

Plan and Solve

Step 1: Choose a Strategy
- Draw a picture.
- Make an organized list.
- Make a table.
- Make a graph.
- Act it out/use objects.
- Look for a pattern.
- Try, check, and revise.
- Write a number sentence.
- Use logical reasoning.
- Solve a simpler problem.
- Work backward.

Step 2: Stuck? Don't give up. Try these.
- Reread the problem.
- Tell the problem in your own words.
- Tell what you know.
- Identify key facts and details.
- Show the main idea.
- Try a different strategy.
- Retrace your steps.

Step 3: Answer the question in the problem.

What strategy can be used? A table can make the problem easier.

Day	Dimes
1	1 dime
2	2 dimes
3	4 dimes
4	8 dimes

$1 + 2 + 4 + 8 = 15$

Answer the problem: Ti will have 15 dimes, or $1.50, after 4 days.

Ti's garden is a rectangle. 6 feet long and 4 feet wide. Ti wants to put stakes 1 foot apart around the edge of the garden. How many stakes does Ti need?

1. Solve the problem. Write the answer in a complete sentence.

_____

21

Intervention Lesson **M11**

Problem-Solving Skill: Plan and Solve (continued)

Solve each problem. Write the answer in a complete sentence.

2. When playing soccer, Sue can wear a red shirt or a white shirt. She can wear black shorts or red shorts. How many different soccer uniforms are possible?

_____

3. Carlos made a pattern out of shapes. He used a red hexagon, then two yellow triangles, then three blue circles, a red hexagon, then two yellow triangles, then three blue circles, and so on, until he used 12 blue circles. How many shapes did he use in all?

_____

4. It costs 25¢ to park for 1 hour. The parking meter can take any combinations of quarters, dimes, and nickels. How many ways can you put 25¢ in this parking meter?

_____

5. Writing in Math For the Parking Meter problem, tell what you know and what you are trying to find.

_____

_____

Test Prep Circle the correct letter for the answer.

6. Which two numbers have a sum of 10 and a difference of 2?

    A 9 and 1   **B** 5 and 5   **C** 7 and 3   **D** 6 and 4

Name _____

Intervention Lesson **M12**

Problem-Solving Skill: Plan and Solve

Example

Kerry is starting a running program. She will run 2 miles each day in January. Then she will increase the amount she runs each day by 2 miles, every 3 months. How far will Kerry be running in a year?

Choose a Strategy
- Draw a picture.
- Make an organized list.
- Make a table.
- Make a graph.
- Act it out/use objects.
- Look for a pattern.
- Try, check, and revise.
- Write a number sentence.
- Use logical reasoning.
- Solve a simpler problem.
- Work backward.

Read and Understand

You know Kerry runs 2 miles each day in January and that she will increase the distance she runs each day by 2 miles every 3 months. You need to find how far Kerry will be running in a year.

Plan and Solve

Which strategy can be used?

Make a table to show the distance each month.

At the end of the year, Kerry will be running 10 miles each day.

Month	Number of Miles
Jan	2
Feb–April	2 + 2 = 4
May–July	4 + 2 = 6
Aug–Oct	6 + 2 = 8
Nov–Dec	8 + 2 = 10

Look Back and Check

Look back at the table and check the answer.

---

1. Meg's family was on vacation. They traveled 150 miles on the first day and then 50 miles each day after that. How many miles did they travel by the end of the fifth day?

   _____

2. Name the strategy used to solve the problem.

   _____

Day	Number of Miles
1	150
2	150 + 50 = 200
3	200 + 50 = 250
4	250 + 50 = 300
5	300 + 50 = 350

23

Name _____

Intervention Lesson M12

Plan and Solve (continued)

3. Jones' Landscape planted some new bushes in the community garden. They planted 4 bushes in the first row. Each row had 1 more bush than the previous row. How many bushes were planted in the fifth row?

   _____

4. Name the strategy used to solve the problem.

   _____

5. Katie spends 50 minutes per week practicing her piano. How many total minutes would she spend practicing her piano over a 15-week period?

   _____

6. Name a strategy to use to solve the problem.

   _____

7. Mr. Thomas was installing a new fence. The fence was in the shape of a rectangle, 50 feet long and 30 feet wide. A post was placed in each corner and every 10 feet in between the corners. How many posts were there? Solve the problem and name the strategy you used.

   _____

Test Prep Circle the correct letter for the answer.

8. Becky surveyed students about their favorite kind of bagel. Which strategy did she use to find the total number of students surveyed?

   $25 + 15 + 5 + 9 = 54$

   A Write an equation
   B Draw a picture
   C Make a table
   D Use objects

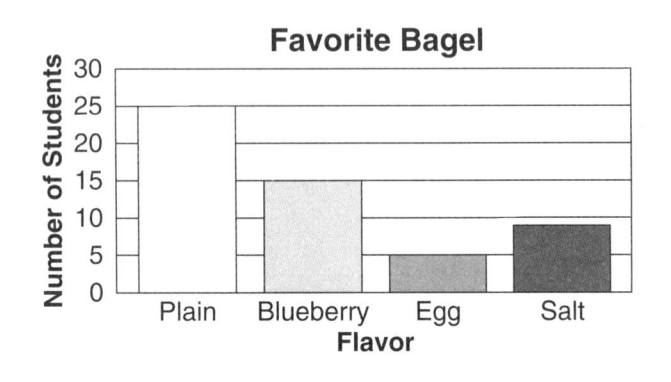

   Favorite Bagel
   (bar graph: Plain 25, Blueberry 15, Egg 5, Salt 9; y-axis: Number of Students; x-axis: Flavor)

Name _____

Intervention Lesson **M13**

Problem-Solving Skill: Look Back and Check

Example

You are not finished with a problem until you look back and check your answer.

Jeff bought a total of 5 seed packets. Jeff bought 2 packets of flower seeds for $2 each and 3 packets of vegetable seeds for $3 each. What is the total cost of the seed packets that Jeff bought?

$2 + $2 + $3 + $3 + $3 = $13

Look Back and Check

Step 1: Check your answer. Yes, I did find the total cost of the seed packets.

Step 2: Check your work. The answer is reasonable. Two packets at $2 each is $4. Three packets at $3 each is $9. $4 + $9 = $13. Addition is the right operation to find a total cost of buying many items.

Kerri solved the Buying Seeds problem by writing the number sentence $2 + $3 = $5. She said the total cost of the packets was $5. Look back and check Kerri's work.

1. Did Kerri answer the right question?

   _____

   _____

2. Is Kerri's work correct? Explain.

   _____

   _____

   _____

25

Name _____

Intervention Lesson **M13**

Math Diagnosis and Intervention System

Problem-Solving Skill: Look Back and Check (continued)

Solve each problem. Write the answer in a complete sentence. Look back and check your work.

3. You get 2 free pencils for each notebook you buy at The School Supply Store. How many free pencils would you get if you bought 4 notebooks?

_____
_____

4. Fran has 30 large shells and 10 small shells. Alan has 40 large shells and 20 small shells. Who has more shells?

_____
_____

5. Writing in Math Choose Question 3 or 4. Tell what strategy you used to solve the problem and explain how you solved it. How did you check that your answer makes sense?

_____
_____
_____

Test Prep Circle the correct letter for the answer.

6. Each of the three shelves have one pair of shoes on them. The colors of the shoes are brown, black, and white. The brown shoes are on the middle shelf. The black shoes are not on the top shelf. On which shelf are the white shoes?

A top shelf   **C** bottom shelf

B middle shelf   **D** top and middle shelves

Intervention Lesson **M14**

Problem-Solving Skill: Look Back and Check

Example

The 270 students at Crestwood School are going on a field trip to the art museum. If the students travel in 6 buses, how many students are on each bus?

Read and Understand

What do I know? 270 students are going. 6 buses are going.

Plan and Solve

Which operation will I need to solve the problem?
Pick a strategy and solve the problem. 270 ÷ 6 = 45
45 students will ride on each bus.

Look Back and Check

Have you checked your answer?

- Check that you answered the right question.
- Check that the answer makes sense.
  50 × 6 = 300, so 45 makes sense.
- Look back and check your work.
- Check that you used the correct operation or procedure.

---

1. A container when empty weighs 150 pounds. If the container is filled with 312 pounds, what is the total weight of the container and its contents? _____

2. Check your work. What operations did you use? _____

Name _____

Intervention Lesson **M14**

Problem-Solving Skill: Look Back and Check (continued)

Allowance Don earned $8 by doing some yard work. He added it to some allowance he had saved and bought a new game for $21.90. Don had $4.15 left over. How much allowance had Don saved?

3. Solve the allowance problem. Give your answer in a complete sentence.

   _____
   _____
   _____

4. Check your answer. What question did you answer?

   _____

5. Why is your answer reasonable?

   _____

6. Check your work. What operations did you use?

   _____

Test Prep Circle the correct letter for the answer.

7. At the school store, Kim bought 8 pens for $0.56 each and 10 pencils for $0.10 each. How much did Kim spend all together?

   A $5.60   **C** $4.48

   B $5.48   **D** $1.00

8. What operations did you use to solve the problem?

   A addition and subtraction

   B multiplication and subtraction

   C addition and division

   D multiplication and addition

Name _____

Math Diagnosis and Intervention System

Intervention Lesson **M15**

Problem-Solving Skill
Translating Words to Expressions

Example

Translating words to a numerical expression can help you solve a problem.

There are 17 Asian elephants and 12 African elephants in the zoo. Write a numerical expression that shows the total number of elephants in the zoo.

The words in the problem give you clues about the operation.

Word or Phrase	Use
Sum; total; increase; together; plus	+
Difference; less than; decrease; minus	−
Product; times; double; twice	×
Quotient; equal groups; shared equally	÷

Read and Understand

There are 17 Asian elephants in the zoo.
There are 12 African elephants in the zoo.

Plan and Solve

Translate words into expressions.

Think: Total of 17 Asian elephants and 12 African elephants
Write: 17 + 12

Look Back and Check

The numerical expression 17 + 12 shows that 12 more than 17 is the total number of elephants in the zoo.

Write the numerical expression for each word phrase.

1. 2 times as many as 4 marbles _____

2. The total of 13 cats and 7 dogs _____

3. $35 decreased by $5 _____

29

Name _____

Math Diagnosis and Intervention System

Intervention Lesson **M15**

Problem-Solving Skill
Translating Words to Expressions (continued)

Write the numerical expression for each word phrase.

4. 12 pennies shared equally by 3 people   _____

5. 25 baseballs minus 3 baseballs   _____

6. The sum of 11 and 24   _____

7. 3 times as many as 2 apples   _____

8. 5 increased by 2   _____

9. 18 less than 30 minutes   _____

10. 10 students separated into 2 equal groups   _____

11. Reasoning If you have 3 fewer quarters than dimes, do you have 3 more dimes than quarters?   _____

Test Prep Which expression matches each word phrase? Circle the correct letter for the answer.

12. $12 less than $20

    A $12 + $20   **C** $12 − $20

    B $20 − $12   **D** $20 × $12

13. 6 groups of birds with 2 birds in each group

    A 6 + 2   **B** 6 − 2   **C** 2 × 6   **D** 6 ÷ 2

Name _____

Intervention Lesson **M16**

Problem-Solving Skill: Translating Words to Expressions

Example

You can use word clues to write algebraic expressions.

Words or Phrases	Operation	Example	Algebraic Expression
sum of plus more than increased by	addition	12 increased by a number	$12 + n$
Minus Difference less than decreased by	subtraction	7 less than a number	$n - 7$
Times Multiplied Product	multiplication	the product of 3 and a number	$3n, 3 \times n$
divided by quotient into	division	the quotient of 12 and a number	$12 \div n$

Write each word phrase as an algebraic expression.

1. 7 added to a number

2. 6 more than the length

3. the quotient of w and 4

4. the product of r and 9

5. the difference of p and 8

6. 8 less than the width

7. the sum of 3 and p

8. the product of 12.4 and y

31

Name _____

Intervention Lesson **M16**

Problem-Solving Skill: Translating Words to Expressions (continued)

Write each word phrase as an algebraic expression.

9. 17 more than a number

10. 6 decreased by a number

11. w divided by 14

12. 7 times r

13. A mile is 5,280 feet. Write an expression to show how many feet $\times$ miles would be.

14. The perimeter of a square equals 4 times the length of a side.

15. You earn $7 per hour. Write an expression to show how much you would earn after h hours.

16. Jason is 4 years older than Tyler. Use t for Tyler's age. Write an expression for Jason's age.

17. **Number Sense** Write two phrases for the expression $w - 12$.

Test Prep Circle the correct letter for the answer.

18. Which expression below shows 7 decreased by a number?

    A $w - 7$ **B** $w + 7$ **C** $7 - w$ **D** $7w$

19. Which is an expression for "six less than w"?

    A $w - 6$ **B** $w + 6$ **C** $6 - w$ **D** $6 \div w$

32

Intervention Lesson **M17**

Problem-Solving Skill: Writing to Explain

Example

You can write to explain an estimate by telling the steps you used.

CDs cost $11 each. DVDs cost $19 each. Do you need more than $20 to buy both a CD and a DVD? Explain how you made your estimate.

Writing a Math Explanation

Write your estimate.   You would need more than $20.

Write your explanation in steps.   Step 1: I rounded $11 to $10 and
                                        $19 to $20. I estimated the cost
                                        of buying a CD and a DVD:
                                        $10 + $20 = $30

                                        Step 2: $30 is more than $20.

Write to explain.

1. Sliced turkey costs $2.89 per pound. Sliced beef costs $3.11 per pound. Marjorie buys 2 pounds of turkey and 1 pound of beef. If she pays for the meat with a $10 bill, will she get change? Explain how you made your estimate.

   _____

   _____

   _____

Intervention Lesson **M17**

Problem-Solving Skill: Writing to Explain (continued)

Write to explain.

2. Explain how the number of eggs changes as the number of dozens changes.

Dozens	1	2	3	4	5
Eggs	12	24	36	48	60

_____

_____

3. A jar of beans is one-third full. There are 47 beans in the jar now. About how many beans would fill the jar? Explain how you made your estimate.

_____

_____

_____

4. **Reasoning** Explain why you can estimate to solve Question 3.

_____

_____

Test Prep Circle the correct letter for the answer.

5. Ramon read 92 pages of a book. Stella read 183 pages of a different book.

   A Stella read about 100 more pages than Ramon.

   B Ramon read about 100 more pages than Stella.

   C Stella read about 10 pages more than Ramon.

   D Ramon read about 10 pages more than Stella.

Intervention Lesson **M18**

Name _____

Problem-Solving Skill: Writing to Explain

Example

Mrs. Barker is making chocolate chip cookies. Her recipe calls for $3\frac{1}{2}$ cups of flour. She does not have enough flour for a full recipe. Write and explain how you would find how many cups of flour are needed to make only half the recipe?

When you write to explain your solution,

- Include the work you did that led to your solution, the steps and operations you used in the order you used them.
- Refer to any diagrams or data that provides important information or supporting details.
- Use words such as "find" and "put" when explaining a process.

1. To find how much flour Mrs. Barker needs, I divided the $3\frac{1}{2}$ cups by 2. $3\frac{1}{2} \div 2 =$
2. Before dividing I estimated $3 \div 2 = 1\frac{1}{2}$
3. I changed $3\frac{1}{2}$ to $\frac{7}{2}$.
4. $\frac{7}{2} \times \frac{1}{2} = \frac{7}{4} = 1\frac{3}{4}$
5. $1\frac{3}{4}$ is close to $1\frac{1}{2}$, so my answer is reasonable.
6. Mrs. Barker would need $1\frac{3}{4}$ cups of flour.

Explain your solution and show your work.

1. Explain how you find the perimeter of the figure shown on the right.

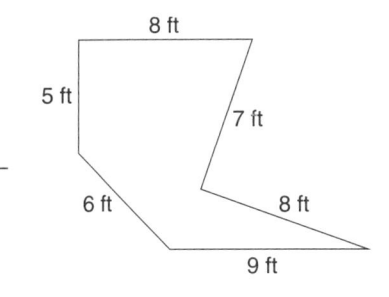

   _____

35

Name _____

Intervention Lesson **M18**

Problem-Solving Skill: Writing to Explain (continued)

Explain your solution and show your work.

2. Manuel went on a 400-mile trip with his friend Julio. If Manuel drove $\frac{3}{5}$ of the trip, how far did he drive?

   _____

   _____

3. Mrs. Kim wants to re-seed a small section of her yard. Explain how to find the area of the yard.

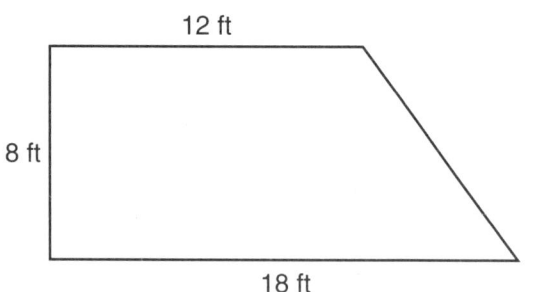

   _____

   _____

   _____

   _____

   12 ft
   8 ft
   18 ft

Test Prep Circle the correct letter for the answer.

4. A jacket regularly priced at $75.00 has been marked down 20%. What is the first step in finding the sale price?

   A Multiply $75 by 20.   **C** Divide $75 by 0.20.

   B Multiply $75 by 0.20.   **D** Divide 20 by 75.

Name _____

Intervention Lesson **M19**

Problem-Solving Skill: Writing to Compare

Example

You can write to compare by looking closely at the data.

The practice schedules for two basketball teams are shown below.

Basketball Practice	Start Time	Water Break	End Time
Team 1	3:00 P.M.	3:50 P.M.	4:00 P.M.
Team 2	4:00 P.M.	4:45 P.M.	5:15 P.M.

Write two statements that compare the data in the schedule.

Writing a Math Comparison

Look closely at the data. How are the data alike? How are they different?

Team 1 starts practice 1 hour earlier than Team 2.

Use words such as "most," "more," and "about the same."

Team 2 has more time for a water break than Team 1 has.

Write to compare.

1. What other comparison statement can you make about the data in the schedule?

   _____

   _____

2. What comparison words did you use to answer Question 1?

   _____

37

Name _____

Intervention Lesson **M19**

Math Diagnosis and Intervention System

Problem-Solving Skill: Writing to Compare (continued)

Write to compare.

3. Use the pictographs below. Write two statements that compare the data on the graphs.

Favorite Snacks of Ms. Low's Class	
Cheese	★ ★ ★
Chips	★ ⌐
Fruit	★ ★ ★ ★
Pretzels	★ ★ ★ ★ ★

Each ★ = 2 votes

Favorite Snacks of Mr. Tan's Class	
Cheese	★ ★ ★
Chips	★
Fruit	★ ★ ⌐
Pretzels	★ ★ ★ ★ ★ ★

Each ★ = 2 votes

_____

_____

_____

_____

Test Prep Circle the correct letter for the answer.

4. Use the bar graphs below. Which comparison statement is true?

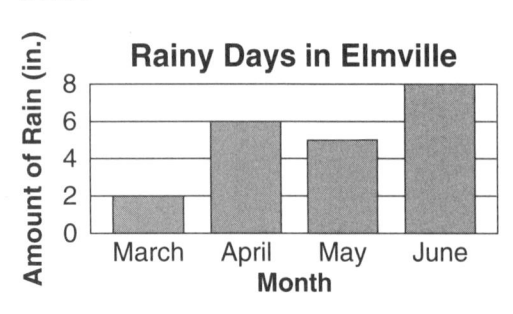

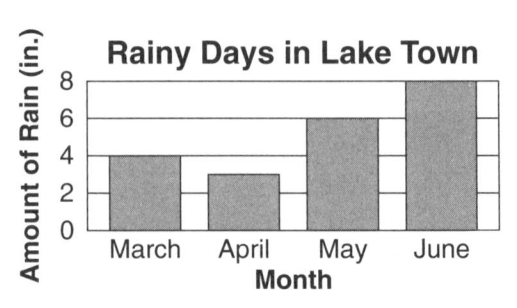

Rainy Days in Elmville
Amount of Rain (in.) — March: 2, April: 6, May: 5, June: 8
Month

Rainy Days in Lake Town
Amount of Rain (in.) — March: 4, April: 3, May: 6, June: 8
Month

A It rained more in Elmville in March than it did in Lake Town.

B It rained more in Lake Town in April than it did in Elmville.

C It rained less in Elmville in May than it did in Lake Town.

D It rained less in Lake Town in June than it did in Elmville.

Name _____

Intervention Lesson **M20**

Problem-Solving Skill: Writing to Compare

Example

When you write to compare, you need to analyze the data and tell how they are alike and different.

The total number of gallons of apple and orange juice sold per day are shown in the line graphs.

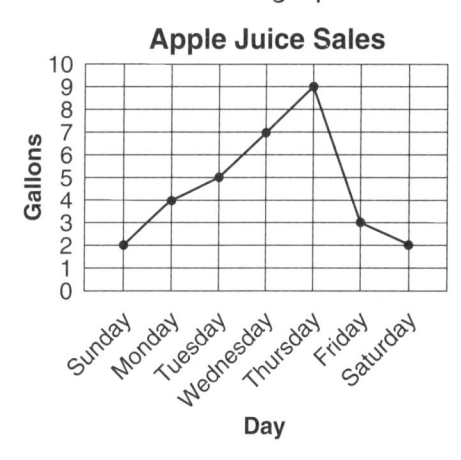

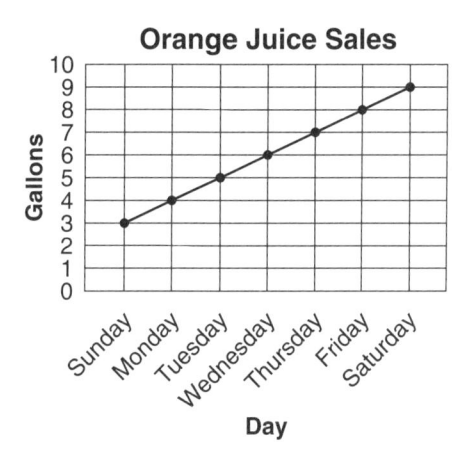

Apple Juice Sales

Orange Juice Sales

You can see that the sales for orange juice increased each day.

You can see that the sale of apple juice decreased from Thursday to Saturday.

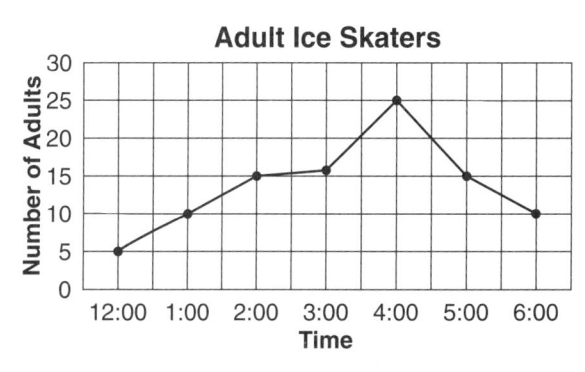

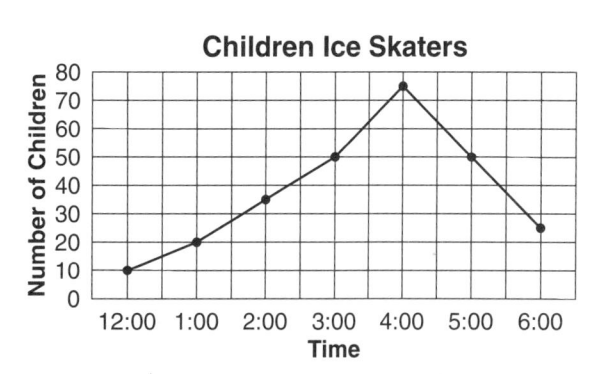

Adult Ice Skaters

Children Ice Skaters

1. Which graph shows the greatest increase in ice skaters between 3:00 and 4:00?

   _____

2. Which graph shows the least amount of skaters at 6:00?

   _____

39

Name _____

Intervention Lesson **M20**

Problem-Solving Skill: Writing to Compare (continued)

3. Write one statement about how the shapes are alike.
_____

_____

4. Write one statement about how the shapes are different.

_____

_____

Patterns Benita and Carol each wrote a number pattern.

Benita's pattern is: 2, 4, 6, 8, 10, 12, 14,…

Carol's pattern is: 1, 3, 5, 7, 9, 11, 13,…

5. Write how the patterns are alike.

_____

6. Write how the patterns are different.

_____

_____

Test Prep Circle the correct letter for the answer.

7. Use the figures to determine which statement is false.
   A Both figures are polygons.
   B Figure A is a regular hexagon.
   C Figure B is a hexagon.
   D Both figures have the same area.

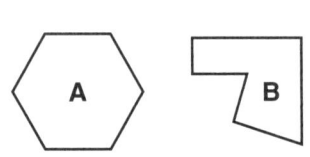

40

Name _____

Intervention Lesson **M21**

Problem Solving Strategy: Writing to Describe

Example

You can write to describe geometric figures by using geometric terms such as *side, edge, face, corner,* and *surface.*

Solid Figures Descriptions of solid figures may mention the number of edges and corners, the number and shape of the faces, whether there are curved surfaces, and whether the solid has the ability to roll.

Use geometric terms to describe how the rectangular prism and the cube are alike.

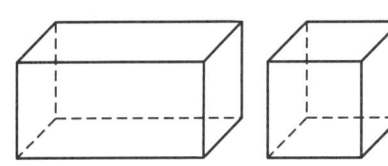

Writing a Math Description

The rectangular prism and the cube both have six faces, twelve edges, and eight corners. They both have all flat surfaces. Neither of them rolls. These two figures are different because the faces of a rectangular prism are not all squares like the faces of a cube.

Rectangular Prism   Cube

Write to describe.

1. Write a statement that describes how the figures at the right are alike.

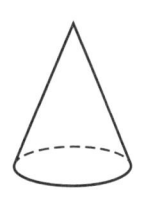

   _____

   _____

   _____

   Cone 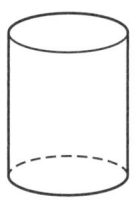   Cylinder

41

Name _____

Intervention Lesson **M21**

Problem Solving Strategy: Writing to Describe (continued)

Write to describe.

2. Write a statement that describes how the box of cereal and the can of soup are different.

   _____
   _____

3. Write a statement that describes how the hexagon and the square are alike.

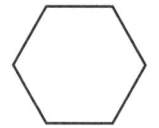

   _____
   _____

4. Write a statement that describes how the hexagon and the square are different.

   _____
   _____

5. **Reasoning** I am a solid figure with six faces, twelve edges, and eight corners. I am not a rectangular prism. What kind of solid figure am I? _____

Test Prep Circle the correct letter for the answer.

6. Use the figures to the right. Which description is true?

   A The pyramid and cube both have eight corners.

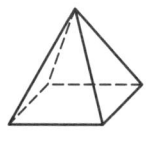

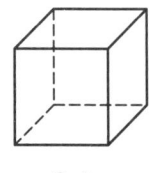

   B The pyramid has five faces, but the cube has six faces.

   C The pyramid and cube can both roll.

   D The pyramid and cube both have twelve edges.

42

Name _____

Intervention Lesson **M22**

Problem-Solving Skill: Writing to Describe

Example

Beth sorted the polygons below into two groups. Use geometric terms to describe the characteristics of each group.

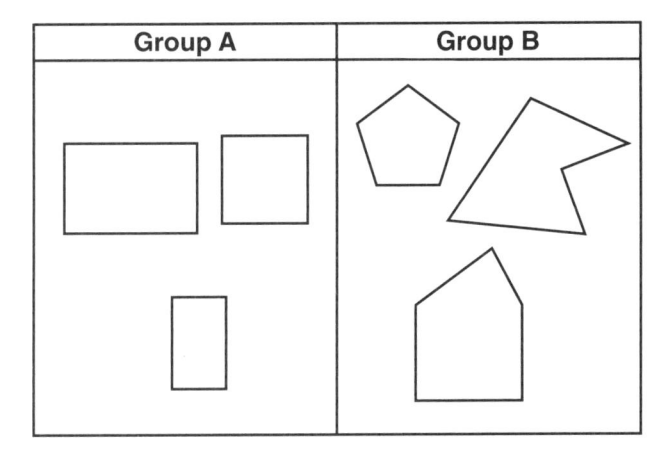

Group A	Group B

You can brainstorm to help you describe the characteristics.

Group A
opposite sides parallel
all figures have 4 sides
all right angles
all the figures have symmetry

Group B
no parallel sides
all figures have 5 sides
all figures have 1 obtuse angle

Be brief when you write your description. Use mathematical terms correctly.

All of the shapes in Group A have 4 sides.

All of the shapes in Group B have 5 sides.

Write a statement that describes the same characteristic for each group above.

_____

_____

43

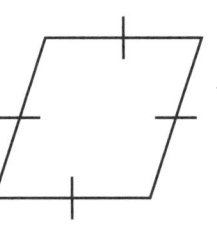

Name _____

Math Diagnosis and Intervention System

Intervention Lesson **M22**

Problem-Solving Skill: Writing to Describe (continued)

Vegetables Picked	
Vegetable	Number
Carrots	
Corn	
Peppers	
Cucumbers	
Broccoli	
Key: each vegetable = 2	

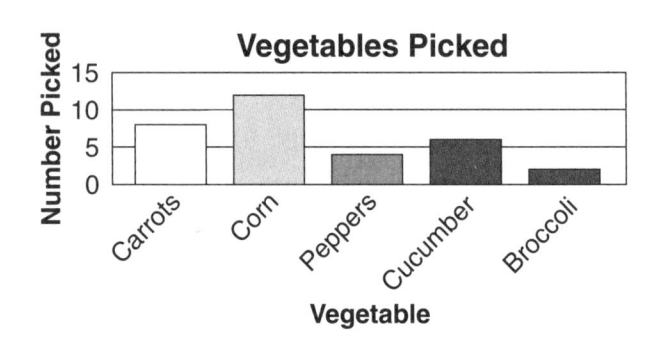

1. Which graph more clearly shows the types of vegetables picked? Which graph more clearly shows the number of each type of vegetable picked?

   _____
   _____
   _____

Use the groups of figures for Questions 2–3.

2. What are some characteristics of Group A?

   _____
   _____
   _____

3. What are some characteristics of Group B?

   _____
   _____

Test Prep Circle the correct letter for the answer.

4. Which is the most complete description of the figure?

   A quadrilateral   **C** parallelogram

   B rhombus   **D** square

44

Name _____

Intervention Lesson **M23**

Problem-Solving Skill
Interpreting Remainders

Example

George has 58 pictures to put in a photo album. Each page in the album will hold 8 pictures. If he fills each page before starting a new page, how many photos will be on the last page?

Read and Understand

Find how many pages will be used.
Find how many pages will be filled completely.
Find how many pictures are on a page that is not completely filled.

Plan and Solve

Divide to find the answer: 58 ÷ 8 = 7 R2
8 pages will be used. 7 pages will be completely filled.
The remainder tells us that there are 2 pictures on the page that is **not** filled.

Look Back and Check

With 8 photos on each page, seven pages will be filled with 56 photos (7 × 8 = 56). One more page is needed to hold the remaining 2 pictures. So, 8 pages will be used to hold the pictures.

Solve. Write the answer in a complete sentence.

1. There are 27 students going to a museum. Each van can hold 6 students. How many vans will be needed?

_____

45

Name _____

Intervention Lesson **M23**

Problem-Solving Skill: Interpreting Remainders (continued)

Solve. Write the answer in a complete sentence.

2. Ed is making stuffed animals. He needs 2 buttons to use as eyes for each animal. If Ed has 15 buttons, how many stuffed animals can he make? How many buttons are left over?

_____

3. Ms. Ramirez is putting 25 fourth-graders into teams of 6 students each. How many teams can she make? How many students are not on a team?

_____

4. Juanita is knitting socks. Each pair of socks needs 3 balls of yarn. She has 20 balls of yarn. How many balls of yarn will not be used?

_____

5. Writing in Math Write a story problem that can be solved using 23 ÷ 5 = 4 R3. Write and explain what the remainder means in your story problem.

_____

_____

_____

Test Prep Circle the correct letter for the answer.

6. Sue has a rock collection. The rocks are stored in cases that each hold 8 rocks. She has 50 rocks. How many cases of rocks does Sue need for her collection?

A 8 cases **B** 7 cases **C** 6 cases **D** 5 cases

Name _____

Math Diagnosis and Intervention System

Intervention Lesson **M24**

Problem-Solving Skill
Interpreting Remainders

Understanding the main idea of a story problem using division can help you to interpret remainders.

Example

Rachel has 108 pictures to put in a photo album. Each page in the album will hold 8 pictures. How many pages will she have to use?

Read and Understand

Find how many pages will be used.
Find how many pages will be filled completely.
Find how many pictures are on a page that is not completely filled?

Plan and Solve

Divide to find the answer: 108 ÷ 8 = 13 R4
14 pages will be used.
13 pages will be completely filled.
There are 4 pictures on a page that is not filled.

Look Back and Check

Thirteen pages will be filled. One more page is needed to hold the remaining four pictures. So, 14 pages will be used to hold the pictures.

Family Vacation The Smith Family is going to vacation in Florida. They are driving 400 miles each day. The trip to Florida is 1,100 miles.

1. How many days will it take to drive to Florida? _____

2. How many full days will they travel? _____

3. How many miles will they travel on the last day? _____

47

Name _____

Intervention Lesson **M24**

Problem-Solving Skill: Interpreting Remainders (continued)

There are 236 people invited to a charity banquet. Each table will seat 8 people.

4. How many tables are needed to seat everyone? _____

5. How many tables can be filled? _____

6. What does the remainder of your answer tell you?

_____

_____

Jon has a rock collection. The rocks are stored in cases that hold 16 rocks in each case. He has 185 rocks in his collection.

7. What is the smallest number of cases that Jon needs to store all the rocks? _____

8. How many cases can Jon completely fill? _____

9. How many rocks are in the case that is not completely filled? _____

Ann invited 10 friends to her birthday party. Her mother ordered 3 extra-large pizzas. One pizza will feed 4 people.

10. Does she have enough pizza for everyone? _____

11. How many complete pizzas will be eaten? _____

12. Will there be any left over, if so, how much? _____

Test Prep Circle the correct letter for the answer.

13. Ross and two friends bought a box of 40 baseballs and divided them equally. How many baseballs did each person get?
    - **A** 10
    - **B** 13
    - **C** 14
    - **D** 12

Name _____

Intervention Lesson **M25**

Problem-Solving Strategy: Draw a Picture

Example

Mr. George is putting a fence along the back of his yard. The wooden fence will be 64 feet long. There will be a post every 8 feet and a post on each end. How many posts will there be?

Read and Understand

What do you know? The fence will be 64 feet long with a post every 8 feet and one on each end.

What are you trying to find? The number of posts Mr. George will need for his fence.

Plan and Solve

What strategy will you use to solve the problem?
Draw a picture to represent the situation and interpret the picture to answer the question.

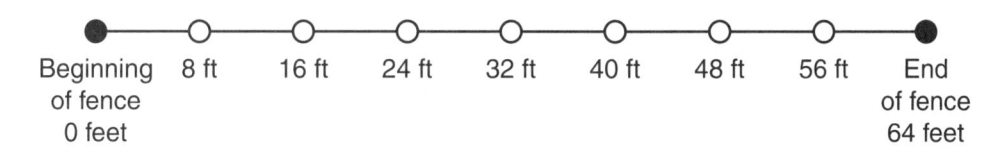

●——○——○——○——○——○——○——○——●
Beginning 8 ft 16 ft 24 ft 32 ft 40 ft 48 ft 56 ft End
of fence   of fence
0 feet   64 feet

Mr. George will need 9 posts for the fence.

Look Back and Check

Step 4: Is your answer reasonable? Yes, all the posts are shown.

Solve each problem. Write the answer in a complete sentence.

1. Gail has a board 15 feet long and wants to cut it into 5 equal pieces, how many cuts will she need to make?

49

Name _____

Intervention Lesson **M25**

Problem-Solving Strategy: Draw a Picture (continued)

Solve each problem. Write the answer in a complete sentence.

2. The cafeteria offers a turkey or ham sandwich on whole wheat, rye or white bread. How many choices of sandwiches are there?

_____

3. You are planting pepper plants in a garden. Your garden is only 48 inches long. The plants must be planted 6 inches apart and the first and last plant must be 6 inches from the edge of the garden. How many plants can you plant in a row?

_____

4. Amy was third in line. Kevin was behind Gina. Meg was behind Amy. If Gina was first, who was second?

_____

5. When a ball bounces, it returns to $\frac{1}{2}$ of its previous height. If Ken drops a ball from 20 feet, how many feet will it have traveled when it hits the ground the second time?

_____

6. Mollie is taller than Kristin and shorter than Mike. Ted is shorter than Mollie but taller than Kristin. Who is the tallest?

_____

Test Prep Circle the correct letter for the answer.

7. Jeff gives himself 4 stamps for each stamp he gives Jack. If Jack has 5 stamps, how many does Jeff have?

    A 5   **B** 8   **C** 16   **D** 20

Name _____

Intervention Lesson **M26**

Problem-Solving Strategy: Draw a Picture

Example

You can draw a picture to help understand and solve many problems. The picture does not need to look like the real thing. It is more like a large symbol.

At lunch, Sara and Jim are third and fourth in line. There are 7 people behind them. How many people are in line?

Read and Understand

What do you know? Sara and Jim are number 3 and number 4 in line. There are 7 people behind them.

What are you trying to find out? The total number of people in line.

Plan and Solve

What strategy will you try? Why? Draw a picture to help you see the problem. You can use something simple, like an X, to stand for people.

X X X X X X X X X X X
    | |
 Sara Jim   7 behind them

Answer: There are 11 people in line.

Look Back and Check

Does your answer make sense? Yes. There are 7 behind and 2 in front. That's 9. Sara and Jim make 2 more for a total of 11.

Complete the picture to solve the problem.

1. A roller coaster has a train of 5 cars that are each 6 feet long. The cars are 2 feet apart. How long is the train?

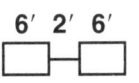

6′ 2′ 6′

The train is _____ feet long.

51

Name _____

Intervention Lesson **M26**

Problem-Solving Strategy: Draw a Picture (continued)

Complete the picture to solve the problem.

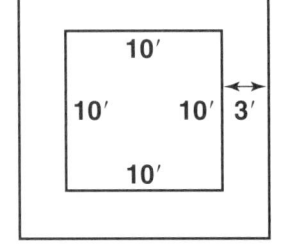

2. A square garden is 10 feet long. A square walkway 3 feet wide goes all the way around the garden. How many feet of fence is needed to go around the walkway?

_____ feet of fence is needed.

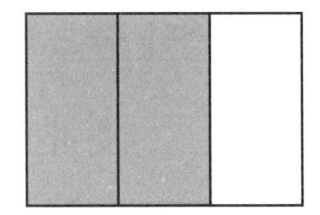

3. Two-thirds of the area of a farm is planted with wheat. The wheat covers 4 acres. What is the area of the farm?

_____

_____

Solve. Draw a picture to help you.

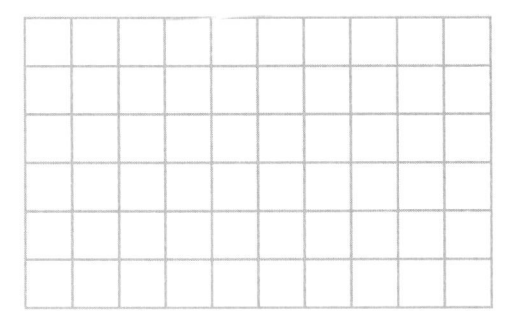

4. You are in a town with square blocks. You walk 5 blocks east, 3 blocks north, then 2 blocks west. How many blocks do you need to walk to get back to your starting point?

_____

_____

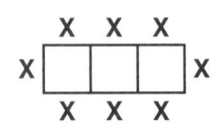

5. Four people can sit at each square table. Three tables are pushed together to form a long rectangular table. How many people can sit at this long table?

_____

Test Prep Circle the correct letter for the answer.

6. A straight fence is 24 feet long. There is a fence post every 6 feet. How many posts are there in the fence?

   A 4   **B** 5   **C** 6   **D** 7

52

Name _____

Math Diagnosis and Intervention System

Intervention Lesson **M27**

Problem-Solving Strategy
Make an Organized List

Example

Terri has homework in English, Reading, Math, and Science. She plans to do Math first. In how many different ways can she arrange the order of her homework?

Read and Understand

What do you know? There is homework in English, Reading, Math, and Science. Math will be done first.

What are you trying to find? Find how many different ways Terri can arrange her homework.

Plan and Solve

What strategy will you use to solve the problem? Make an organized list with Math listed first.

Math, English, Reading, Science
Math, English, Science, Reading
Math, Reading, English, Science
Math, Reading, Science, English
Math, Science, English, Reading
Math, Science, Reading, English

There are six different ways.

Look Back and Check

Is your answer reasonable? Yes, Math is first and the order is different for each way.

---

1. Max, June, and Greg are posing for a picture. If they stand in one row, how many different ways can they pose?

   _____

53

Name _____

Intervention Lesson **M27**

**Problem-Solving Strategy
Make an Organized List** (continued)

Solve each problem.

2. At a jewelry store, you can have your purchase gift-wrapped in silver, gold, or red paper with a white, pink, or blue ribbon. You can choose one color of paper and one color of ribbon. How many gift-wrap combinations are available?

_____

3. Mr. Johnson is making sandwiches. He has wheat bread and rye bread. He has ham and salami. He also has colby and cheddar cheese. Each sandwich will have one kind of bread, one kind of meat, and one kind of cheese. How many different kinds of sandwiches can he make?

_____

4. Leslie has a penny, a nickel, and a dime in her pocket. If she picks out 2 coins, what amounts of money could she get?

_____

5. Each child at Heather's party has chosen a sandwich and a drink. If there are 7 children at the party, can they each have a different lunch?

Sandwiches	Drinks
Turkey Ham Tuna Peanut butter	Milk Juice

_____

Test Prep Circle the correct letter for the answer.

6. Paul, Steve, and Bridget get on an elevator. The boys want to be polite and let Bridget go first. In how many different ways can they arrange their order to get on the elevator?

  A 1   **B** 2   **C** 3   **D** 9

Name _____

Intervention Lesson **M28**

Problem-Solving Strategy: Make an Organized List

Example

You can make a list to help you keep track of possibilities. Use a pattern to organize your list so you don't leave anything out and don't list anything twice.

You are going to record 3 of your favorite songs on a CD. How many different orders are there for you to choose from?

Read and Understand

What do you know?   There are 3 songs. Use each song once.

What are you trying to find out?   The number of possible orders for 3 songs.

Plan and Solve

What strategy will you try? Why?   **Strategy: Make an Organized List** It will help me keep track of different orders.

- You can use a different symbol, such as a letter or number, to stand for each song.
- If you start with song A, the other 2 songs can only be in 2 orders, BC or CB.

orders starting with song A	orders starting with song B	orders starting with song C
ABC	BAC	CAB
ACB	BCA	CBA

Answer: There are 6 possible orders.

Complete the organized list to solve the problem.

1. When ordering a fruit dessert at a café, you need to choose 2 scoops of fruit. The menu lists strawberries, blackberries, and cherries. The scoops can be the same or different. How many types of dessert can be ordered?

    There are _____ possible desserts.

55

Name _____

Math Diagnosis and Intervention System

Intervention Lesson **M28**

Problem-Solving Strategy: Make an Organized List (continued)

Complete each list to solve the problems.

2. One spinner has the numbers 1, 2, and 3. The other has 3, 4, and 6. You spin each and multiply the two numbers to get your score. How many different scores are possible?

   There are _____ possible different scores.

   $1 \times 3 = 3$

   $1 \times 4 = 4$

   $1 \times 6 =$ _____

   $2 \times$ _____ = _____

   _____ $\times$ _____ = _____

   _____ $\times$ _____ = _____

   _____ $\times$ _____ = _____

   _____ $\times$ _____ = _____

   _____ $\times$ _____ = _____

3. You have black pants and tan pants. You have 3 shirts: black, red, and green. How many different outfits can you make?

   B—B _____

   B—R _____

   B—G _____

   _____

Solve. Try making an organized list to help you.

4. You throw 2 darts and multiply the 2 numbers you hit to get your score. A dart that misses the board counts as zero. How many different scores are possible?

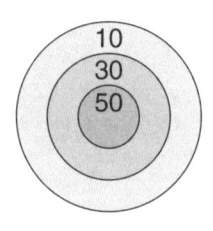

   10
   30
   50

   _____
   _____
   _____
   _____

Test Prep Circle the correct letter for the answer.

5. For $9.99, you get a pizza with your choice of 2 different toppings. The toppings—sausage, pepperoni, and mushrooms—are put on in any order. How many pairs of different toppings are there?

   A 3   **B** 4   **C** 6   **D** 8

Name _____

Intervention Lesson **M29**

Problem-Solving Strategy: Make a Table

Example

Ann and Jane began reading the same book on the same day. If Ann reads 8 pages each day and Jane reads 5 pages each day, what page will Jane read on the day that Ann reads page 40?

Read and Understand

What do you know? Ann reads 8 pages per day and Jane reads 5 pages per day.

What are you trying to find? What page Jane will be reading when Ann is reading page 40.

Plan and Solve

What strategy will you use to solve the problem? Make a table. Jane will be reading page 25.

Day	1	2	3	4	5	6
Ann's Page	8	16	24	32	40	48
Jane's Page	5	10	15	20	25	30

Look Back and Check

Step 4: Is your answer reasonable? Yes, the table shows that on day 5 Ann is on page 40 and Jane is on page 25.

Complete the table. Solve each problem.

1. Rebecca must put 4 eggs in each basket. There are 8 baskets. How many eggs does she need? _____

Number of Baskets	1	2	3	4	5	6	7	8
Number of Eggs	4	8						

57

Name _____

Intervention Lesson **M29**

Problem-Solving Strategy: Make a Table (continued)

Complete the table and solve each problem. Write the answer in a complete sentence.

2. Martin needs to water each tree with 3 gallons of water. How many gallons of water will he need for 7 trees?

Number of trees	1	2	3	4	5	6	7
Gallons of water							

_____

_____

3. Diego recorded the height of a bean plant. The first week, the plant was 2 inches high. The second, third, and fourth week, it was 4 inches, 6 inches, and 8 inches high. At this rate, when will the bean plant be 12 inches high?

Week	1	2	3	4	5	6	7
Height							

_____

_____

Test Prep Circle the correct letter for the answer.

4. Sam waters his lawn every 6 days. Beth waters her lawn every 8 days. If they both water their lawns today, in how many days will they both be watering their lawns together again?

  A 48 days **C** 20 days

  B 24 days **D** 14 days

Intervention Lesson **M30**

Problem Solving Strategy: Make a Table

Example

You are making a bulletin board display of 21 drawings. If you put them in a triangular pattern, how many rows will the drawings make?

Read and Understand

What do you know? 21 drawings will form a triangle. Each row has 1 more drawing than the row above it.

What are you trying to find out? The number of rows the pattern will have.

Plan and Solve

What strategy will you try? Why? Make a Table to help keep track of drawings and rows.

Row	1	2	3	4	5	6
Drawings in the Row	1	2	3	4	5	6
Total Drawings Used	1	3	6	10	16	21

Make the table as long as you need.

The drawings can make 6 rows.

Look Back and Check

Does your answer make sense? Yes. Each row has one more picture than the previous row.

Solve the problem.

1. You need $\frac{3}{4}$ of a cup of milk to make 8 pancakes. How many pancakes can you make with $4\frac{1}{2}$ cups of milk?

   You can make _____ pancakes.

59

Name _____

Intervention Lesson **M30**

Math Diagnosis and Intervention System

Problem-Solving Strategy: Make a Table (continued)

Complete the table to solve the problem.

2. You have $23 and will save $7.50 each week. In how many weeks will you have enough money to buy a $68 DVD player?

Weeks	0	1	2			
Savings	$23.00	$30.50	$38.00	$45.50		

I will have enough money in _____ weeks.

3. Each quilt square has 2 red sections and 3 blue sections. If 18 blue sections are used, how many red sections are needed?

squares						
red sections						
blue sections						

4. You get paid $0.75 for each card you make. Your friend gets $2 per hour plus $0.25 for each card. How many cards do you need to make each hour to make the same pay as your friend?

Cards made in 1 hour				
my pay				
friend's pay				

Test Prep Circle the correct letter for the answer.

5. Each box lunch has 3 cookies and 4 baby carrots. If 15 cookies are used to make some box lunches, how many baby carrots are used?

  A 12   **B** 15   **C** 20   **D** 24

60

Name _____

Intervention Lesson **M31**

Math Diagnosis and Intervention System

Problem-Solving Strategy: Make a Graph

Example

The table lists the types of books Abby read over the summer. How many more fiction books did she read than science fiction?

Type of Book	Number
Mystery	5
Science fiction	2
Nonfiction	3
Fiction	7
History	4

Read and Understand

You know the number of books Abby read.

You need to find how many more fiction books Abby read than science fiction books.

Plan and Solve

Make a graph to solve the problem. A bar graph helps to compare data.

Abby read 5 more fiction books than science fiction books.

Look Back and Check

Look back and check to see if the answer is reasonable.

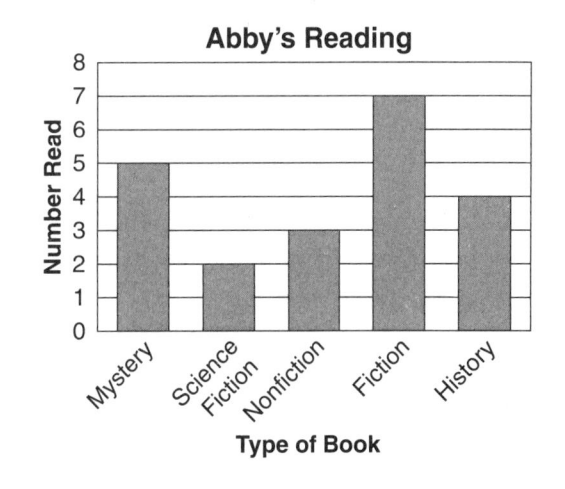

Solve. Write the answer in a complete sentence.

1. Use the graph above to answer the question. How many books did Abby read all summer?

   _____

2. How many more fiction books did Abby read then history books?

   _____

61

Name _____

Intervention Lesson **M31**

Problem-Solving Strategy: Make a Graph (continued)

Solve. Write the answer in a complete sentence.

Greg took a survey of the number of third-grade runners at three schools in his town.

School	Number of Runners
Fairfield	12
Lincoln	20
Park	18

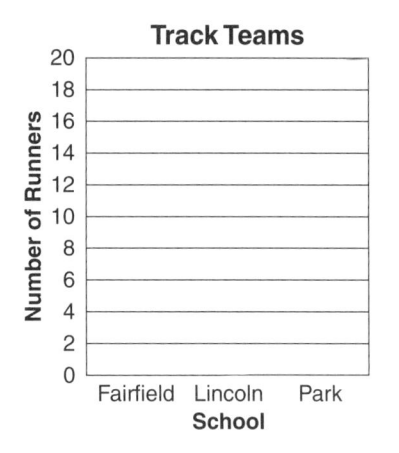

3. Draw the bars in the graph.

4. Which school has the most runners?

_____

5. How many runners are there in total at all three schools?

_____

6. The table shows the number of people visiting different zoo animals. Make a bar graph of the data.

Animal	Number of Visitors
Monkeys	20
Polar Bears	32
Reptiles	15
Lions	24
Fish	12

Test Prep Circle the correct letter for the answer.

7. How many more people visited the monkeys than the fish?

    A 6   **B** 8   **C** 10   **D** 12

Name _____

Intervention Lesson **M32**

Math Diagnosis and Intervention System

Problem-Solving Strategy: Make a Graph

A graph can help you see patterns in data.

Jeremy recorded the height of a plant for five days. On what day did the plant grow the most?

Day	Height
Monday	4 cm
Tuesday	5 cm
Wednesday	8 cm
Thursday	10 cm
Friday	15 cm

Read and Understand

What do you know? The height of the plant on each day.

What are you trying to find out? On what day did the plant grow the most?

Plan and Solve

What strategy will you try? Make a Graph to help you see how the plant's height changes.

The plant grew the most on Friday.

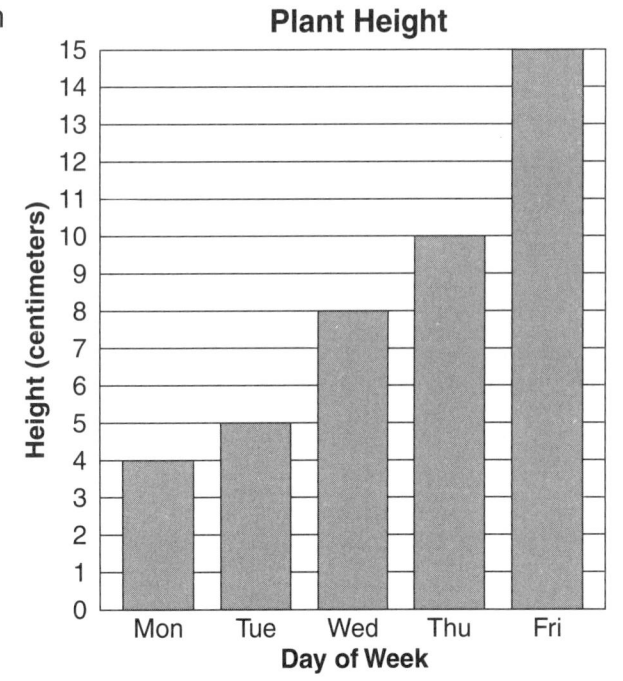

Plant Height

(Bar graph showing Height in centimeters by Day of Week: Mon 4, Tue 5, Wed 8, Thu 10, Fri 15)

Look Back and Check

Does your answer make sense? Yes. The plant grew 5 centimeters on Friday which is more than on any other day.

63

Name _____

Intervention Lesson **M32**

Problem-Solving Strategy: Make a Graph (continued)

Use the graph in the Example to solve the problem.

1. On what day did the plant grow the least?

   _____

2. On what day did the plant grow past the 9-centimeter mark?

   _____

Make a graph with the data in the table to answer Questions 3–5.

| Oak School Students |||
Grade	Girls	Boys
1	30	20
2	70	50
3	60	30
4	50	30
5	60	40

3. In which grade is there the greatest difference between the number of boys and the number of girls?

   The greatest difference is in grade _____.

4. In which grade is there the least difference between the number of boys and the number of girls?

   The least difference is in grade _____.

Test Prep Circle the correct letter for the answer.

5. Which of the following is true?
   - **A** The number of girls is larger than boys in all grades.
   - **B** The number of boys is the same as girls in Grade 5.
   - **C** The number of girls in Grade 3 is the same as in Grade 4.
   - **D** The number of girls in Grade 1 is the same as in Grade 2.

Name _____

Intervention Lesson **M33**

Problem Solving Strategy: Use Objects

Example

You can use objects to model, or act out, some problems.

A board is divided into four sections. Two sections will be painted gray and two sections will be painted white. How many different patterns are possible?

Read and Understand

What do you know?	The board is divided into 4 equal sections. There are two colors.
What are you trying to find out?	The number of different patterns to paint the board.

Plan and Solve

• You can use a strip of paper to represent the board and shade sections of it with pencil.	The top two boards can be turned to match each other, so they are not really different but are the same pattern. The same is true of the bottom two boards.

Answer: There are 4 possible color combinations.

1. How can you cut a double-layer cake into 8 pieces with only 3 straight cuts? Hint: Use two pieces of paper to represent the two layers of the cake.

_____
_____
_____

65

Name _____

Intervention Lesson **M33**

Problem Solving Strategy: Use Objects (continued)

Use objects to finish solving the problem.

2. Six children form a triangle. How can they turn the triangle upside down if only two of the children move? Draw two arrows on the picture to show your answer.

3. You are making a toddler's toy with 2 large red beads and 2 large blue beads on a ring. In how many different orders can you arrange the beads?

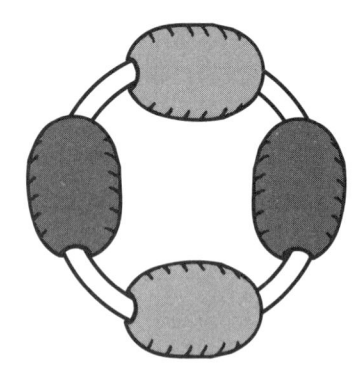

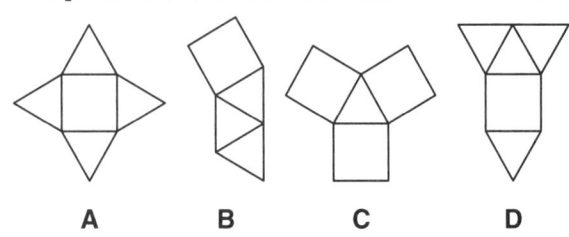

Test Prep Circle the correct letter for the answer.

   A   B   C   D

4. Which pattern can be folded to form a square pyramid?

   A A   **B** B   **C** C   **D** D

66

Name _____

Intervention Lesson **M34**

Problem-Solving Strategy: Act It Out

Example

Wanda carries a stack of 17 books. Lyle carries a stack of 11 books. How many books should Wanda give Lyle so they carry the same number?

Read and Understand

What do you know? Wanda has 17 books. Lyle has 11 books.

What are you trying to find? Find the number of books that Wanda should give Lyle, so they have the same number.

Plan and Solve

What strategy will you use to solve the problem? Act it out by placing 17 books in one pile and 11 books in another pile. Move one book at a time from Wanda's pile to Lyle's pile until they are equal.

When Wanda gives one to Lyle, she will have 16 and Lyle will have 12. When she gives him a second book, she will have 15 and Lyle will have 13. When she gives him a third book, they will both have 14 books. Wanda should give Lyle 3 books.

Look Back and Check

Is your answer reasonable? Yes, the piles of books are now equal.

Solve each problem. Write the answer in a complete sentence.

1. Bill, Phillip and Mandy each have 7 baseball cards. Suppose Bill gives 3 of his to Phillip, and Phillip gives 2 of his to Mandy. How many cards does Phillip have? _____

67

Name _____

Intervention Lesson **M34**

Problem-Solving Strategy: Act It Out (continued)

Solve each problem.

2. David wants to make a flower garden by enclosing it with landscape timbers. If a landscape timber is 8 ft long, and he has 6 timbers, what is the maximum area of garden space he can enclose?

   _____

3. A sporting goods store would like to display a new line of tennis balls in a triangular stack. The bottom row will have 7 canisters and each row going up will have one less canister. How many canisters will be on display? _____

4. The Harris children collect snow globes. Jill has 5, Brad has 7, and Tracey has 6, but 3 of hers broke when the family moved. If Mrs. Harris asks the children to share the snow globes equally, how many will each child get? _____

5. The Oak Street Theater has 4 sections of seating. Each section has 5 rows of seats. Two sections have 4 seats in each row. The other sections have 3 seats in each row. How many seats are there in the theater? _____

6. Jeremy and Frank both collect trading cards. Jeremy has enough allowance to buy 6 each week and Frank's parents allow him to buy 4 each week. How many trading cards will Jeremy have when Frank has 36? _____

Test Prep Circle the correct letter for the answer.

7. Andrew folds a sheet of paper in half 5 times. When he opens it up, how many sections will there be?

   A 40 **B** 32 **C** 16 **D** 8

Name _____

Intervention Lesson **M35**

Problem-Solving Strategy: Look for a Pattern

Example

What will the next picture of dots look like?

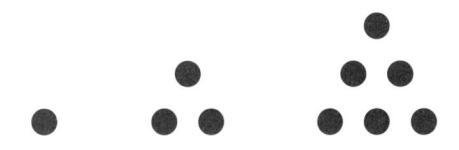

•   • • •   • • • •

Read and Understand

What do you know? The number of dots in each picture or row.
What are you trying to find? How the next picture of dots will look.

Plan and Solve

What strategy will you use? Look for a pattern.
There are 2 more dots in the second picture than in the first picture.
There are 3 more dots in the third picture than in the second picture.
The number of dots added to the picture, increases by 1 each time.

There will be 4 more dots in the next picture.

Look Back and Check

Is your answer reasonable? Yes, the number of dots added increases by 1 each time.

Complete the pattern.

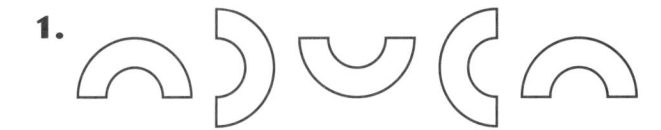

1. ∩ ⊃ ∪ ⊂ ∩

Name _____

Intervention Lesson **M35**

Problem-Solving Strategy: Look for a Pattern (continued)

2. What letter comes next in the pattern?

DEEDEEDEEDE

_____

3. What are the next two numbers in the pattern 7, 10, 17, 20, 27, 30?

_____

4. Paul lives at 413 Market Street. Pete lives next door at 411 Market Street, and Ted lives next door to Pete at 409 Market Street. Matt lives two doors down from Pete. What is Matt's address?

_____

5. Describe the pattern.

_____

6. Amanda received 3 new customers on her paper route in January. In February, she received 6 new customers. In March, she received 9 new customers. If this pattern continues, how many new customers should she expect to receive in May?

_____

Test Prep Circle the correct letter for the answer.

7. What are the next two numbers in the pattern?
12, 17, 22, 27, 32, 37, …

A 38, 39   **B** 40, 45   **C** 47, 57   **D** 42, 47

8. What are the next two numbers in the pattern 50, 48, 46, 44, 42, 40?

A 52, 53   **B** 38, 36   **C** 39, 37   **D** 40, 36

Name _____

Intervention Lesson **M36**

Math Diagnosis and Intervention System

Problem-Solving Strategy: Look for a Pattern

Solve problems by finding a pattern and extending it.

The floor of a hotel lobby will have a growing pattern of square tiles. If the pattern continues, how many tiles will be in the sixth design?

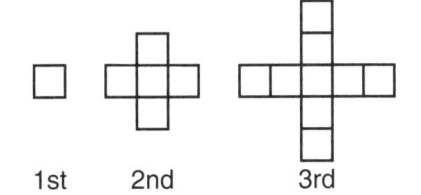

1st   2nd   3rd

Read and Understand

What do you know? In each design, a square is added to each side.
What are you trying to find? The number of tiles in the sixth design.

Plan and Solve

What strategy will you try? Look for a Pattern.
4 tiles are added each time. So the pattern is "add 4."

1st   2nd   3rd   4th   5th   6th

1 tile 5 tiles 9 tiles 13 tiles 17 tiles 21 tiles
   +4   +4   +4   +4   +4

Keep adding 4 until you get to the sixth design.
There will be 21 tiles in the sixth design.

Look Back and Check

Does your answer make sense? Yes. If you add five 4s to 1, you get 21.

Complete the pattern to solve the problem.

1. A marching band is making a triangle formation; Row 1 has 1 marcher, Row 2 has 2 marchers, and so on. How many marchers are needed to make the triangle 10 rows deep?

   _____ marchers are needed.

   1st 2nd 3rd 4th 5th 6th 7th 8th 9th 10th
    1   3   6   10   15   21   28   36   45   55
      +2   +3   +4   +5   +6   +7   +8   +9 +10

71

Problem-Solving Strategy: Look for a Pattern (continued)

Complete the pattern to solve the problem.

2. The rectangular tablecloth has a repeating pattern. How many squares on the whole tablecloth are gray?
   _____

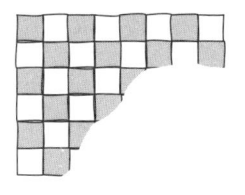

3. What are the missing numbers in the pattern?

   $4\overline{)9}$ = 2 R1 $4\overline{)10}$ = 2 R2 $4\overline{)11}$ = 2 R3 $4\overline{)}$ = 3

Solve. Try looking for a pattern to help you. Use the division problem for Questions 4–6.

$7\overline{)386}$ = 55 R1

4. Without dividing, what is 387 ÷ 7? _____
5. Without dividing, what is 385 ÷ 7? _____
6. Without dividing, what is 384 ÷ 7? _____

Test Prep Circle the correct letter for the answer.

7. Which time comes next in the pattern?

   12:05   12:30   12:55

   A 12:20   **B** 1:05   **C** 1:20   **D** 1:55

72

Intervention Lesson **M37**

Problem-Solving Strategy
Try, Test, and Revise

Example

Ellie bought 1 bracelet and 1 charm. The bracelet cost twice as much as the charm. If Ellie spent $0.36, what was the cost of the charm?

Read and Understand

What do you know? Ellie spent $0.36 on 1 bracelet and 1 charm. The bracelet was twice as much as the charm.

What are you trying to find? Find the cost of 1 charm.

Plan and Solve

What strategy will you use? Try, check, and revise

1st Try	2nd Try	3rd Try
Charm: $0.10 Bracelet: $0.20 Total: $0.30	Charm: $0.11 Bracelet: $0.22 Total: $0.33	Charm: $0.12 Bracelet: $0.24 Total: $0.36
Not enough. Revise the price up 1¢.	Not enough. Revise the price up 1¢.	Correct!

Ellie bought the charm for $0.12 and the bracelet for $0.24.

Look Back and Check

Is your answer reasonable? Yes, the sum is $0.36.

Try, check, and revise to solve the problem.

1. Don has 10 sports cards in all. He has 2 more baseball cards than football cards. How many of each card does he have?

73

Name _____

Intervention Lesson **M37**

Math Diagnosis and Intervention System

Problem-Solving Strategy: Try, Test, and Revise (continued)

Use the data in the table for Questions 2–4.

Camping Town	
Sleeping bag	$10
Flashlight	$3
Lantern	$5
Canteen	$4
Dried food	$2

2. Karen bought 2 different items. She spent $8. Which items did she buy?

   _____

3. Jake bought 3 different items. He spent a total of $15. Which items did he buy?

   _____

4. Adam spent $19 at Camping Town on 4 items. Two of his items were the same. What did he buy?

   _____

5. Gina has twice as many goldfish as zebra fish. Together, there are 42 of these fish in her tank. How many goldfish and zebra fish does she have?

   _____

6. Josh delivers pizza. In his money pouch are 6 bills worth $18. If he only has $1 and $5 bills, how many of each bill does he have?

   _____

Test Prep Circle the correct letter for the answer.

7. Mr. Gray's class has 24 students. He has three times as many girls as boys in the class. How many girls are in the class?

   A 6   **B** 10   **C** 16   **D** 18

Name _____

Intervention Lesson **M38**

Math Diagnosis and Intervention System

Problem Solving Strategy
Try, Test, and Revise

Suppose you don't know how to find an answer directly, but you do know how to tell if an answer is correct. You can keep trying and checking different answers as you work toward the correct one.

Example

The area of a rectangular garden is 60 square feet. The garden's perimeter is 38 feet. What are its dimensions?

Read and Understand

What do you know?	The garden is a rectangle. Area = 60 sq ft, Perimeter = 38 ft
What are you are trying to find?	The length and width of the rectangle.

Plan and Solve

What strategy will you try? Why?	Strategy: Try, Test, and Revise
	I can tell when I get the answer by seeing if the area and perimeter are what they are supposed to be.
• Try a length and width that have a product of 60.	Try **6** and **10**: Area = 6 × 10 = 60 Perimeter = 6 + 6 + 10 + 10 = 32 **no**
• Start with numbers that are easy to work with.	Try **5** and **12**: Area = 5 × 12 = 60 Perimeter = 5 + 5 + 12 + 12 = 34 **no**
• If the perimeter is not 38, try again.	Try **4** and **15**: Area = 4 × 15 = 60 Perimeter = 4 + 4 + 15 + 15 = 38 ✓
	The garden is 15 ft long and 4 ft wide.

Look Back and Check

Does your answer make sense? Yes. The area is 60 sq ft and the perimeter is 38 ft.

75

Intervention Lesson **M38**

Problem Solving Strategy: Try, Test, and Revise (continued)

Complete the solution.

1. The sum of two numbers is 96. Their quotient is 3. What are the two numbers?

    Try **90** and **6**:   Sum = 90 + 6 = 96

    _____ and _____   Quotient = 90 ÷ 6 = 15 **no**

2. There are 12 figures. Some are triangles and the rest are rectangles. The figures have 45 sides in all. How many of each type of figure are there?

Triangles	Rectangles	Total Sides
10	2	(10 × 3) + (2 × 4) = 38, too low

Solve. Try, Test, and Revise to help you.

3. Simone bought 20 CDs and paid $149. How many new and how many used CDs did she buy?

    CDs
    New $12 each
    Used $5 each

4. The perimeter of a rectangular poster is 120 in. The length of the poster is three times its width. What are the dimensions of the poster?

5. A group spent $180 for 11 tickets. How many adult tickets and how many child tickets did the group buy?

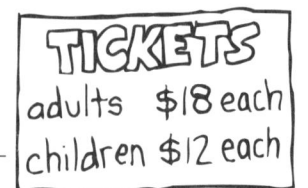

    TICKETS
    adults $18 each
    children $12 each

6. A group of hexagons and pentagons has a total of 73 sides. There are 14 figures in the group. How many of each type of figure are in the group?

Test Prep Circle the correct letter for the answer.

7. The sum of 4 consecutive numbers is 66. What are the numbers?

    A 63, 64, 65, 66   **C** 12, 13, 14, 15

    B 15, 16, 17, 18   **D** 6, 10, 20, 30

Name _____

Intervention Lesson **M39**

Problem-Solving Strategy
Write a Number Sentence

Example

For a school bake sale, you would like to make brownies and cupcakes. How many eggs do you need to make both treats?

Bake Goods	Number of Eggs
Brownies	3
Cookies	2
Cupcakes	2

Read and Understand

What do you know? You need 3 eggs to make brownies and 2 eggs to make cupcakes.

What are you trying to find? The total number of eggs you need to make both recipes.

Plan and Solve

What strategy will you use to solve the problem? Write a number sentence. Let e stand for the total number of eggs you need to make both treats. Solve for e.

$e = 3 + 2$

You will need 5 eggs for both recipes.

Look Back and Check

Is your answer reasonable? Yes, 3 eggs + 2 eggs = 5 eggs.

Solve each problem. Write your answer in a complete sentence.

1. Mr. and Mrs. Gordon have 11 grandsons and 5 granddaughters. How many grandchildren do the Gordons have?

_____

Name _____

Intervention Lesson **M39**

Problem-Solving Strategy
Write a Number Sentence (continued)

2. Maggie wants to buy a set of paints for her art class. The cost of the paints is $49. She has saved $17 from her allowance so far. How much more money does she need to buy the set of paints?

3. Mr. Kerr wants to buy circus tickets for his family. Tickets cost $7 each. How much will it cost to buy 6 tickets?

4. Amy and Todd have blown up 34 balloons for a birthday party. Amy has blown up 18 balloons. How many did Todd blow up?

5. The McKay family needs to drive 212 miles to reach the beach for a family vacation. If they have traveled 85 miles, how many more miles do they need to travel?

6. There are 56 students signed up for a dance class at Jarvis Dance studio. The students are divided into groups of 8. How many groups are in the dance class?

Test Prep Circle the correct letter for the answer.

7. The Bulldogs basketball team scored 38 points in the first half of the game. In the second half of the game the team scored 46 points. How many points did the Bulldogs score in the entire game?

   A 12   **B** 61   **C** 74   **D** 84

Name _____

Intervention Lesson **M40**

Math Diagnosis and Intervention System

Problem Solving Strategy: Write an Equation

You can write an equation to show how the parts of a problem go together. Then you can solve the problem by solving the equation.

Example

If you travel at 40 miles per hour, how long will it take you to go 180 miles?

Read and Understand

What do you know?	You go 40 miles each hour.
What are you are trying to find?	How much time will it take to go 180 miles.

Plan and Solve

What strategy will you try? Why?	Write an Equation. It can help me see what operation to use.
Write a word equation. Put in the numbers you know.	number of hours × number of miles per hour = number of miles, or number of hours × 40 = 180
Use a letter for what you don't know. Solve the equation to find the unknown value.	$n \times 40 = 180$ $n \times 40 \div 40 = 180 \div 40$ $n = 4.5$
State the answer.	It will take 4.5 hours to go 180 miles.

Complete the solution.

1. A book and a $2.75 magazine cost $14.50 together. How much does the book cost?

79

Problem Solving Strategy: Write an Equation (continued)

Complete the solution.

2. Charlotte bowled 3 games. Her average score was 142. What was her total for the 3 games together?

    average score = total score ÷ number of games

    _____

Solve. Try writing an equation to help you.

3. Phillip paid $18.75 for a soccer ball on sale. What was the price before the sale? _____

4. Tammy earns $8 per hour. She earned $480 last month. How many hours did she work? _____

5. The perimeter of a square is 70 inches. What is the length of each side? _____

Test Prep Circle the correct letter for the answer.

6. Allen forgot to record the amount of a check that he had written. Before he wrote it, his bank balance was $132.50. Afterwards, his balance was $78.80. What was the amount of the check?

    A $101

    B $78.80

    C $20.00

    D $53.70

Name _____

Intervention Lesson **M41**

Problem-Solving Strategy
Use Logical Reasoning

Example

Helen, Paula, and Tammy go to a baseball game. They bought popcorn, a hotdog, and a taco for a snack. None of the girls ate food that begins with the same letter as her name. Paula did not eat a taco. Who ate which snack?

Read and Understand

What do you know? Three girls attended a baseball game and each had a snack.

What are you trying to find? Find the snack each girl ate.

Plan and Solve

What strategy will you use to solve the problem? Use logical reasoning. Make a chart with the information you are given. Helen had the taco, Paula had the hotdog, and Tammy had the popcorn.

	Helen	Paula	Tammy
Popcorn	No	No	Yes
Hotdog	No	Yes	No
Taco	Yes	No	No

Look Back and Check

Is your answer reasonable? Yes, the information led to the right conclusions.

Use logical reasoning to solve the problem.

1. Nancy is thinking of a number. It is between 52 and 64. It does not have a 5 in the tens place. The sum of its digits is 9. _____

81

Name _____

Intervention Lesson **M41**

Problem-Solving Strategy: Use Logical Reasoning (continued)

Use logical reasoning to solve each problem.

2. Abby, Bill, Cara, and Dick have dentist appointments today. Each appointment is 30 minutes long. Abby's appointment is at 10:30. Bill's appointment is the last one before lunch. Cara's appointment is 1 hour after Dick's. What time is Dick's appointment? What time is Cara's?

_____

3. Gary, Neil and Kyle just finished their lunch. One of the boys had a ham sandwich, another had a turkey sandwich, and the third, a chicken sandwich. Use the clues to find who ate what for lunch?

	Gary	Neil	Kyle
Ham			
Turkey		yes	
Chicken			

Kyle is allergic to ham.

Neil did not have the chicken.

Gary always eats ham.

_____

4. The spring concert will be in May. Complete the calendar to find the date of the spring concert.

The concert will be on a weekend.

The date of the concert has 2 digits.

The sum of the digits is 3.

May						
S	M	T	W	TH	F	S
1	2	3	4	5	6	7
8	9	10	11	12	13	14
15	16	17	18	19	20	21
22	23	24	25	26	27	28
29	30	31				

_____

Test Prep Circle the correct letter for the answer.

5. Joey is thinking of a number between 25 and 35. A 3 is not in the tens place. Joey's number is not even, and it is not 27.

A 25   **B** 26   **C** 28   **D** 29

Name _____

Intervention Lesson **M42**

Problem-Solving Strategy
Use Logical Reasoning

Example

Sometimes you can solve a problem by organizing the possibilities and then eliminating all but one of them.

> The avocet, gerenuk, and koi are three animals. The gerenuk has no wings. The koi has no feathers and is not warm-blooded. Which animal is the bird, which is the mammal, and which is the fish?

Read and Understand

What do you know? The gerenuk has no wings, and the koi has no feathers. Therefore, neither is a bird. The koi is not warm-blooded.

What are you are trying to find? Which is a bird, a fish, and a mammal?

Plan and Solve

What strategy will you try? Use logical reasoning to help eliminate choices until only one choice is left. Make a table to show what you eliminate.

Neither the gerenuk nor koi is a bird, so the avocet must be the bird.

The koi is not a mammal, so the gerenuk must be a mammal.

The koi is the only animal that can be a fish.

	bird	fish	mammal
avocet	yes	no	no
gerenuk	no	no	yes
koi	no	yes	no

Look Back and Check

Does your answer make sense? Yes. The answer fits all the clues.

83

Name _____

Math Diagnosis and Intervention System

Intervention Lesson **M42**

Problem Solving Strategy: Use Logical Reasoning (continued)

Use logical reasoning to finish the table and solve the problem.

1. The name of one of the four countries has the same number of letters as the name of its capital. The capital of Nigeria does not start with the letter N. There are half as many letters in Chad as in its capital. Which city is the capital of which country?

	Lagos	Luanda	Nairobi	Ndjamena
Angola	no	**yes**	no	no
Chad		no		
Kenya		no		
Nigeria		no		

_____ is the capital of Angola.

_____ is the capital of Chad.

_____ is the capital of Kenya.

_____ is the capital of Nigeria.

2. Drake, Emily, and Flo get to school in different ways. One rides the bus, one walks, and one goes by car. Emily doesn't ride. Drake goes with 30 other children. Who gets to school which way?

	Bus	Car	Walk
Drake			
Emily			
Flo			

Test Prep Circle the correct letter for the answer.

3. A breakfast cereal has 3 shapes: circle, square, and star. Each shape is a different color: green, red, or yellow. The green and red shapes have corners. The star is not red. Which color is the square?

   A green   **B** red   **C** yellow   **D** can't tell

Name _____

Intervention Lesson **M43**

Math Diagnosis and Intervention System

Problem-Solving Skill: Solve a Simpler Problem

Example

Mr. Lange cut a 25-foot rope into 12 equal-sized pieces. How many cuts did he make?

Read and Understand

What do you know? Mr. Lange has a 25-foot rope that he cut into 12 equal pieces.
What are you trying to find? How many cuts did he make?

Plan and Solve

What strategy will you use to solve the problem?
Solve simpler problems to find an answer.

How many cuts divide a 4-foot rope into 2 equal pieces? 1 cut
How many cuts divide a 6-foot rope into 3 equal pieces? 2 cuts
How many cuts divide a 10-foot rope into 5 equal pieces? 4 cuts

There is 1 less cut then the number of equal pieces needed.

It will take Mr. Lange 11 cuts to make 12 equal-size pieces.

Look Back and Check

Is your answer reasonable? Yes, 11 cuts is less than the number of equal pieces.

Solve each problem. Write the answer in a complete sentence.

1. Suppose Mr. Lange had a rope 50 feet long and wanted to cut it into 25 equal pieces. How many cuts would it take?

_____

85

Name _____

Intervention Lesson **M43**

Problem-Solving Skill: Solve a Simpler Problem (continued)

Use the soccer information for Questions 2–5.

The Washington Stars signed up for a single elimination soccer tournament. This means that 2 teams play and the loser is eliminated. There are 8 entries in the tournament.

2. How many games would be played if 2 teams entered? _____

3. How many games would be played if 3 teams entered? _____

4. How many games would be played if 4 teams entered? _____

5. How many games must be played to determine the champion? _____

---

6. Six people at a party all shake hands with each other. How many handshakes is that?

   _____

   _____

7. During the grand opening of a craft store, every fourth customer was given a discount coupon. Every tenth customer was given a discount coupon and a gift. During the grand opening, 120 people visited the store. How many coupons and gifts were given away?

   _____

Test Prep Circle the correct letter for the answer.

8. Mr. Cintron needs to cut a 20-foot length of rope in half. Each length will then be cut into 5 equal lengths. How many equal lengths of rope will there be in total?

   A 4 **B** 5 **C** 10 **D** 20

Name _____

Intervention Lesson **M44**

Math Diagnosis and Intervention System

Problem-Solving Strategy: Solve a Simpler Problem

Example

You can solve a hard problem by solving a simpler one first.

Suppose you divide a rectangle with 10 straight lines. What is the greatest number of sections you can form?

Read and Understand

What do you know? Use 10 straight lines to divide a rectangle.
What are you trying to find? The greatest number of sections that you can form.

Plan and Solve

What strategy will you try? Solve simpler problems by finding how many pieces you can make with 1 line, 2 lines, or 3 lines.

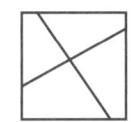

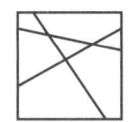

1 line, 2 pieces   2 line, 4 pieces   3 line, 7 pieces

Lines	1	2	3	4	5	6	7	8	9	10
Pieces	2	4	7	11	16	22	29	37	46	56

+2 +3 +4 +5 +6 +7 +8 +9 +10

Extend the pattern to 10 lines.
56 is the greatest number of pieces.

Look Back and Check

Does your answer make sense? Yes. Every time a line crosses another line, it forms sections. Each new line you draw makes more new sections.

87

Intervention Lesson **M44**

Problem-Solving Strategy: Solve a Simpler Problem (continued)

Complete the pattern to solve the problem.

1. You are making octagons by gluing together 6 red toothpicks and 2 blue toothpicks. How many different octagons can you make?

   You can make _____ different octagons.

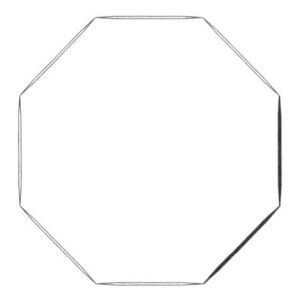

   It's simpler to think of different ways to arrange the 2 blue sides than the 6 red sides.

2. How many squares are there in a 4-by-4 grid of squares?

   There are _____ squares.

   1 unit square

   4 unit squares
   1 2x2 square

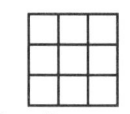

   9 unit squares
   4 2x2 squares
   1 3x3 square

Solve. Try solving a simpler problem to help you.

3. What is $25 \times 2.76 \times 4$?

4. What is $\frac{2}{3} \times 4\frac{5}{8} \times \frac{3}{2}$?

5. The square is 3 cm long. Each rectangle is 2 cm by 1 cm. What is the area of the entire figure?

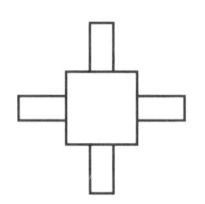

Test Prep Circle the correct letter for the answer.

6. You are making hexagons by gluing together 4 blue toothpicks and 2 green toothpicks. How many hexagons can you make that look different in color patterns?

   A 6   **B** 4   **C** 3   **D** 2

Name _____

Intervention Lesson **M45**

Problem-Solving Strategy: Work Backward

Example

Jean cuts 30 inches off a board to make a shelf. Then she cuts the rest of the board into 4 equal pieces. Each piece is 6 inches long. How long was the original board?

Read and Understand

What do you know? A board was cut into pieces; 1 piece is 30 inches long, and 4 pieces are each 6 inches long.

What are you trying to find? The length of the board before it was cut.

Plan and Solve

What strategy will you use to solve the problem? Work backward to find the answer. Add the lengths of all the pieces to find the length of the board before it was cut. Start with the last piece of information you know.

$$\underbrace{6 + 6 + 6 + 6}_{\text{4 pieces}} + \underbrace{30}_{\text{1 piece}} = 54$$

The original board was 54 inches long.

Look Back and Check

Is your answer reasonable? Yes, I worked backward using the lengths of the pieces.

Solve each problem.

1. Jeb bought a CD for $14.99 plus $1.19 for tax. He had $3.82 left. How much money did he have before he bought the CD?

_____

Name _____

Intervention Lesson **M45**

Problem-Solving Strategy: Work Backward (continued)

Solve each problem.

2. Lola took 45 minutes to get ready for school. She walked to school in 20 minutes and then waited 5 minutes before the bell rang at 8:55 A.M. What time did she get out of bed that morning?

_____

3. Josh picked a number. Next, he added 14, subtracted 6, and added 3. He ended with 34. What number did he pick?

_____

4. There were 7 people in a bus. At the next stop, 4 women got in and 4 men got out. Of the 7 people in the bus, $\frac{4}{7}$ were women. How many women were in the bus to start?

_____

5. The trip from your home to the museum takes 45 minutes. You need 1 hour and 30 minutes to tour a special exhibit in the museum. You want to finish the tour before 3:00 P.M. What is the latest time you should leave home to go to the museum?

_____

Test Prep Circle the correct letter for the answer.

6. You currently have $15 in your savings account. When you started saving a few months ago, you decided to save $3 each month. It is now August 1. What month did you start saving?

A February   **B** March   **C** April   **D** May

90

Name _____

Intervention Lesson **M46**

Problem-Solving Strategy: Work Backward

These directions tell you how to get from the park to the library. How do you get from the library to the park?

| 1. Go 3 km East. |
| 2. Turn right. |
| 3. Go 2 km South. |
| 4. Turn left. |
| 5. Go 1.5 km. |

Read and Understand

What do you know? Directions from the park to the library.

What are you trying to find? Directions from the library to the park.

Plan and Solve

What strategy will you try? Work Backward to get to the park.

The steps forward are:

park → 3 km E → turn right → 2 km S → turn left → 1.5 km E → library

Start at the end and work backward. Use the opposite direction. Change right to left, East to West, North to South.

library → 1.5 km W → turn right → 2 km N → turn left → 3 km W → park

Look Back and Check

Does your answer make sense? Yes. You can sketch a map to check the directions.

Complete the solution.

1. Pat cut $3\frac{3}{4}$ in from a wooden rod. Then he cut the rod in half. Each half was $2\frac{1}{2}$ inches long. How long was the rod before he cut it?

$(n - 3\frac{3}{4}) \div 2 = 2\frac{1}{2}$

$2\frac{1}{2} \times \underline{\hspace{1cm}} + 3\frac{3}{4} = n$

The rod was _____ inches long.

$n = \underline{\hspace{1cm}}$

91

Name _____

Intervention Lesson **M46**

Problem-Solving Strategy: Work Backward (continued)

Complete the solution.

2. The movie starts at 1:15 P.M. It takes 25 minutes to get ready and 15 minutes to get there. Then it takes 5 minutes to buy a ticket and get a seat. When is the latest you should start getting ready?

   Start time + 25 min. + 15 min. + 5 min. → 1:15 P.M.

   _____

3. A store reduced the price of a DVD player by $15. A week later, all prices in the store were cut in half for a clearance sale. The clearance price of the DVD player was $47. What was the original price?

   $(n - 15) \div 2 = 47$

   _____

Solve.

4. Kirk doubled a recipe for brownies. When he mixed the ingredients, he reduced the sugar by $\frac{1}{2}$ cup to make the brownies less sweet. He used $1\frac{1}{2}$ cups of sugar. How many cups of sugar did the original recipe call for?

   _____

5. Ana spent half her savings on a pair of skates. Then she spent $12 on a CD. If she earned $5 and now has $65, how much money did she have before she bought the skates?

   _____

Test Prep Circle the correct letter for the answer.

6. What is the mystery number?

   Subtract 8 from the mystery number.
   Multiply by 3.
   Add 8.
   The result is 41.

   A 19   **B** 22   **C** 107   **D** 11

Intervention Practice **M1**

Problem-Solving Skill: Choose an Operation

Circle the correct letter for the answer.

1. Ellie has 8 shells. Alonzo has 3 times as many shells as Ellie. How many shells does Alonzo have?
   A 83
   B 24
   C 11
   D 5

2. Jimmy earns $3 for an hour of babysitting. He earns $5 for painting the fence. How much will Jimmy make if he baby-sits for 5 hours?
   A $8
   B $10
   C $15
   D $25

3. Ms. Jackson drove 105 miles on Wednesday and 67 miles on Thursday. Which operation must you use to find how many more miles Ms. Jackson drove on Wednesday than on Thursday?
   A addition
   B subtraction
   C multiplication
   D division

Use the data in the table for Questions 4–5.

| Votes for Class President ||
Student	Number of Votes
Karen	5
Jake	10
Jorge	13
Mia	6
Paul	7

4. How many more votes did Jorge get than Karen?
   A 13 votes
   B 8 votes
   C 5 votes
   D 4 votes

5. Betty received 4 times as many votes as Mia. How many votes did Betty receive?
   A 24 votes
   B 28 votes
   C 40 votes
   D 400 votes

Name _____

Intervention Practice **M2**

Problem-Solving Skill: Choose an Operation

Circle the correct letter for the answer.

1. Ruth has a ribbon 18 feet long. If she cuts 8 feet off, how much of the ribbon does she have left?

   A 36 feet   **C** 10 feet
   B 26 feet   **D** 8 feet

2. Which operation will you use to solve the following problem? A large pizza is cut into 10 slices. Dani and her four friends share the pizza equally. How many slices did she eat?

   A add   **C** multiply
   B subtract   **D** divide

Use the table for Questions 3–4.

Item	Cost per package
$\frac{1}{4}$-inch washers	$0.68
$\frac{1}{4}$-inch nuts	$1.29
2-inch bolts	$1.79
4-inch bolts	$1.99

3. Chris is building a doghouse. He bought 1 package of $\frac{1}{4}$-inch nuts and 1 package of 2-inch bolts. About how much was the total cost of his items?

   A $2.00   **C** $4.50
   B $3.00   **D** $5.75

4. Abi gave the clerk a $10.00 bill for a package of 4-inch bolts. About how much change did she get?

   A $2.00   **C** $6.00
   B $4.00   **D** $8.00

5. Katie has a strip of fabric $12\frac{1}{2}$ feet long. She cuts off a piece $5\frac{1}{2}$ feet long to make a tail for a kite. How many feet of fabric are left?

   A $5\frac{1}{2}$ feet   **C** $6\frac{1}{2}$ feet
   B 7 feet   **D** 18 feet

6. Which operation will you use if you want to solve the following problem in one step? Mr. Carter earns $28 per hour. How much does he earn if he works for $6\frac{1}{2}$ hours?

   A add   **C** multiply
   B subtract   **D** divide

Intervention Practice **M3**

Problem-Solving Skill: Multiple-Step Problems

Circle the correct letter for the answer.

1. George bought 2 T-shirts, and Ellen bought 3 T-shirts. The T-shirts cost $7 each. What hidden question can you use to find how much they spent?

   A What is the cost of 10 T-shirts?
   B How many more T-shirts did Ellen buy than George?
   C What color are the T-shirts?
   D How many T-shirts did they buy altogether?

2. Sue is 8 years old. Fred is 3 years older than Sue. Jenna is 4 years older than Fred. How old is Jenna?

   A 11 years old   C 16 years old
   B 15 years old   D 44 years old

3. Mr. Smith bought 2 pounds of bananas and 4 pounds of apples. The fruit cost $2 for each pound. How much did Mr. Smith spend on fruit?

   A $4   C $12
   B $8   D $18

Use this table to answer Questions 4–5.

Prices for Bags of Pet Food	Dog	Cat
Small	$2	$1
Medium	$4	$2
Large	$6	$3

4. What is the total cost of 2 small bags of cat food and 1 large bag of cat food?

   A $2   C $7
   B $3   D $5

5. How much more do 2 medium bags of dog food cost than 2 medium bags of cat food?

   A $4   C $12
   B $8   D $16

6. Lena caught 8 fish, and Sven caught 2 fish. The fish weighed about 2 pounds each. What hidden question can you use to find how much the fish weighed in all?

   A What is the weight of all the fish?
   B How many more fish did Lena catch than Sven?
   C What kind of fish did they catch?
   D How many fish did they catch altogether?

Intervention Practice **M4**

Problem Solving Skill: Multiple-Step Problems

Circle the correct letter for the answer.

1. Mrs. Ling buys 6 identical pairs of athletic socks for $5.75 per pair. Tax is $2.07. If she pays with a $100 bill, how much is her change?

   A $65.50   C 36.57
   B $63.43   D $34.50

2. The Hannula family is going to the movies at 5:00. Movie tickets cost $7 for adults and $5 for children under the age of 12. What hidden question can you use to find how much it will cost for 4 adults and 3 children to go to the movies?

   A What time are the Hannula's attending the movie?
   B What is the total cost of a child and adult ticket?
   C How many of each kind of ticket are there?
   D How many more adult tickets than children's tickets are purchased?

Use the table for Questions 3–4.

Cathy's Pet Grooming		
Type of Service	Mon–Thurs	Fri. or Sat.
Bath/wash	$5	$7
Bath and dry	$7	$9
Haircut	$10	$12
Toenails	$3	$5

3. Mrs. Riggs has 2 dogs that she wants bathed. How much will she save by taking the dogs on Wednesday instead of Friday?

   A $2   C $5
   B $4   D $6

4. Mr. Lee wants a haircut, toenail trimming, and a bath for his poodle. He wants his Labrador to have only a bath. How much will he pay if he takes both dogs on Saturday?

   A $31   C $17
   B $24   D $12

5. Jorie bought 4 pairs of pants. Ira bought 3 pairs of pants. Each pair of pants cost $21.99. What hidden question can you use to find how much they spent?

   A What is the cost of 8 pairs of pants?
   B How many more pairs of pants did Jorie buy than Ira?
   C What type of pants did Jorie buy?
   D How many pairs of pants did they buy?

6. Etta bought 40 feet of edging for her flower garden. The 3 pieces she used to edge her roses were 5.5 feet, 9 feet, and 12.5 feet long. How much edging was left?

   A 27 feet   C 13.3 feet
   B 18 feet   D 13 feet

Name _____

Intervention Practice **M5**

Problem-Solving Skill
Extra or Missing Information

Circle the correct letter for the answer.

1. Asim's room is 12 feet long and 10 feet wide. The family room is 14 feet wide. What information do you need to find how much longer the family room is than Asim's room?

   A the length of Asim's room
   B the length of the family room
   C the width of Asim's kitchen
   D the width of Sue's room

2. Marvin, Alvin, and Billy are brothers. Marvin is 10 years old. Alvin is 2 years younger than Marvin. Billy is 3 years older than Marvin. What extra information is not needed to find how old Billy is?

   A How much younger Alvin is than Marvin.
   B How old Marvin is.
   C How much older Billy is than Marvin.
   D All information is needed.

3. There will be 8 people at Lila's party. Each person will get 1 glass of juice. Juice costs $2 per carton. Each carton fills 4 glasses. How many cartons of juice will Lila need?

   A 1 carton   C 4 cartons
   B 2 cartons   D 32 cartons

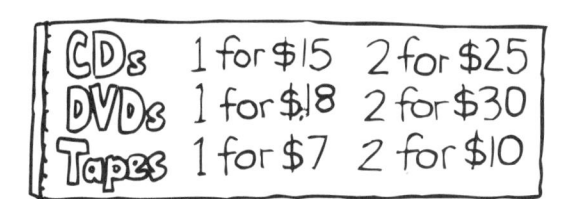

```
CDs    1 for $15   2 for $25
DVDs   1 for $18   2 for $30
Tapes  1 for $7    2 for $10
```

Use the sign for Questions 4 and 5.

4. Tyrone bought 3 CDs and 2 tapes. How much did he pay for the CDs?

   A $15   C $30
   B $25   D $40

5. Brittany bought some DVDs and some tapes. She spent $40 in all. Her change was $10. How many DVDs and tapes did Brittany buy?

   A 2 DVDs and 2 tapes
   B 3 DVDs and 2 tapes
   C 2 DVDs and 3 tapes
   D 2 DVDs and 4 tapes

Name _____

Intervention Practice **M6**

Problem-Solving Skill
Extra or Missing Information

Circle the correct letter for the answer.

1. Megan bought 4 toys for the children she babysits. Each toy cost the same amount of money. Megan received $4.15 in change. How much did each toy cost?

   A $3.25
   B $5.25
   C $12.10
   D not enough information

2. Adam collects postcards. He collected 12 postcards on his last vacation. Some of the cards cost $1.00, and some cost $1.25. He spent a total of $13. How many $1.25 postcards did he buy?

   A 4
   B 8
   C 12
   D not enough information

3. Jo is 54 inches tall and weighs 114 pounds. Her brother, Leroy, is 2 inches taller and weighs 18 pounds more. How much does Leroy weigh?

   A 142 pounds
   B 132 pounds
   C 96 pounds
   D not enough information

4. What extra information is given?

   Mr. Eric's class is going on a field trip to the science museum. Admission tickets to the museum cost $6.00. Lunch costs $3, and a snack costs an additional $1. The class has raised enough money to pay for the $175 bus rental fee. How much will it cost each student?

   A The cost of admission to the museum is $6.00.
   B The cost of lunch is $3.00.
   C The cost of a snack is $1.00.
   D The cost to rent the bus is $175.

5. How much will it cost each student in Mr. Eric's class to go on the field trip in Question 4?

   A $4   C $8
   B $6   D $10

6. A builder purchased 4 sheets of plywood and 12 rolls of insulation for a total of $127. Each sheet of plywood cost $25.00. What was the cost of each roll of insulation?

   A $2.25
   B $2.50
   C $3.00
   D not enough information

Name _____

Intervention Practice **M7**

Problem-Solving Skill: Exact or Estimate?

Circle the correct letter for the answer.

1. For which problem is an estimate enough?

   A On Saturday, 368 people went to the zoo. On Sunday, 406 people went. Did at least 900 people go that weekend?

   B On Saturday, 368 people went to the zoo. On Sunday, 406 people went. How many people went that weekend?

   C On Saturday, 368 people went to the zoo. On Sunday, 406 people went. How many fewer people went to the zoo on Saturday than on Sunday?

   D On Saturday, 368 people went to the zoo. On Sunday, 406 people went. How many more people went to the zoo on Sunday than on Saturday?

2. Carl is playing a computer game. The top score is 500 points. Carl's score so far is 199. How many more points does Carl need to reach the top score?

   A exactly 201 more
   B exactly 301 more
   C at least 400 more
   D at least 500 more

3. Box A weighs 183 pounds. Box B weighs 124 pounds. Which sentence is true?

   A Box A weighs more than 100 pounds more than Box B.
   B Box B weighs at least 50 pounds less than Box A.
   C Box B weighs exactly 10 pounds more than Box A.
   D Box A weighs exactly 29 pounds less than Box B.

4. A new computer costs $885. Ms. Richards has saved $598. How much more money does Ms. Richards need to buy the computer?

   A at least $1,483 more
   B at least $900 more
   C exactly $300 more
   D exactly $287 more

Name _____

Intervention Practice **M8**

Problem-Solving Skill: Exact or Estimate?

Circle the correct letter for the answer.

1. Jane used a 9-foot piece of material to make scarves. Each scarf is 2 feet long. How many scarves could she make?

   A 2 scarves
   B 3 scarves
   C 4 scarves
   D 5 scarves

2. Choose the situation where you expect an exact answer.

   A The amount of money deposited into a bank account.
   B The number of berries growing on a plant.
   C The number of people sitting in the stands at a high school basketball game.
   D The number of seeds needed to plant in a garden.

3. An acre contains 43,560 square feet. Mr. Jefferson's lot measures 200 feet long and 60 feet wide. About what part of an acre does he own?

   A $\frac{1}{4}$ acre
   B $\frac{1}{2}$ acre
   C $\frac{3}{4}$ acre
   D 1 acre

4. Choose the situation where you expect an estimate.

   A The number of points scored in a soccer game.
   B The number of toes on a bird.
   C The number of gallons of water in a large swimming pool.
   D The cost of two movie tickets.

5. One bag of fertilizer will cover 5,000 square feet. How many bags will Patricia need to fertilize a field that measures 200 feet by 300 feet?

   A 20 bags
   B 15 bags
   C 12 bags
   D 10 bags

Name _____

Intervention Practice **M9**

Problem-Solving Skill: Read and Understand

Circle the correct letter for each answer.

1. Emily bought 2 CDs for $7 each. She bought 1 CD for $10. How much did Emily pay for the CDs?
   A $7
   B $14
   C $24
   D $34

2. In January, it snowed on 12 days. In February, it snowed on 19 days. On how many more days did it snow in February than it did in January?
   A 31 days
   B 30 days
   C 7 days
   D 6 days

3. Tanesha tossed a penny several times. The penny landed on heads 20 times. It landed on tails 30 times. How many times did Tanesha toss the penny?
   A 60 times
   B 50 times
   C 10 times
   D 3 times

4. The gas tank in Mr. Rivera's car holds 16 gallons of gas. There are 8 gallons of gas in the tank now. How many more gallons does Mr. Rivera need to put into the tank to fill it?
   A 2 gallons
   B 8 gallons
   C 14 gallons
   D 24 gallons

5. Mia collected 15 red marbles and 9 black marbles. She put 10 of the red marbles and 5 of the black marbles in a bag. How many marbles were in the bag?
   A 40 marbles
   B 20 marbles
   C 24 marbles
   D 15 marbles

6. There are 12 months in a year. Each month has a certain number of letters. Which month has the fewest letters?
   A September
   B July
   C June
   D May

Problem Solving Skill: Read and Understand

Circle the correct letter for the answer.

Use the information for Questions 1–2.

Buffy's Books sells hardback books for an average of $25 each and paperback books for an average of $6 each. Buffy buys the hardback books for an average of $18 each and the paperback books for an average of $3.50 each.

1. About how much profit is made on a paperback book?

   A $3.50   C $2.50
   B $3.00   D $2.00

2. In June, Buffy's sold 2,000 hardback books. How much profit did Buffy's make on these books?

   A $7,000   C $14,000
   B $12,000 D $50,000

3. Some tortoises have been known to live over 150 years. Tortoises range in size from the Madagascan spider tortoise, which at adulthood is about 10 cm long, to the Aldabra giant tortoise, which can be up to 1.4 m long. What is the difference in size between the largest and smallest tortoise?

   A 8.6 cm   C 140 cm
   B 130 cm   D 150 cm

Use the table for Questions 4–6.

School Supplies	
Pencils	10 for $1.00
Paper	$0.79
Pen	$1.25
Paste	$1.29
Folders	4 for $1.00

4. Suzan bought 10 pencils, 2 packs of paper, and 1 bottle of paste. How much did Suzan spend on school supplies?

   A $12.87   C $3.87
   B $5.02   D $3.08

5. Mark bought 1 pack of paper, 2 pens, 1 bottle of paste, and 8 folders. How much did he spend on school supplies?

   A $6.58   C $4.48
   B $5.58   D $3.29

6. If Mark gave the clerk a $10 bill, how much change did he get back?

   A $6.71   C $4.42
   B $5.15   D $3.42

Name _____

Intervention Practice **M11**

Problem-Solving Skill: Plan and Solve

Circle the correct letter for the answer.

1. Beth has 16 baseball cards. She wants to have 25 baseball cards. How many more cards does Beth need?

   A 41 cards
   B 31 cards
   C 10 cards
   D 9 cards

2. Ellie has been doing homework for 15 minutes. The time now is 4:20 P.M. At what time did Ellie start doing her homework?

   A 4:35 P.M.
   B 4:25 P.M.
   C 4:05 P.M.
   D 4:00 P.M.

3. Each box of pencils contains 10 pencils. Each carton contains 6 boxes of pencils. How many pencils are in 5 cartons?

   A 10 pencils
   B 60 pencils
   C 300 pencils
   D 3,000 pencils

4. Jackie is thinking of a number. When she adds 3 to her number and then subtracts 1 from the total, she gets 5. What number is Jackie thinking of?

   A 1   C 3
   B 2   D 4

5. Sue and Sam borrow some books from the library. Sam borrows twice as many books as Sue. Sue borrows 5 books. How many books does Sam borrow?

   A 5 books
   B 10 books
   C 20 books
   D 25 books

6. George's local swimming pool is 50 feet long. George swims for 150 feet. How many lengths of the pool is that?

   A 50 lengths
   B 10 lengths
   C 3 lengths
   D 2 lengths

Name _____

Intervention Practice **M12**

Problem-Solving Skill: Plan and Solve

Circle the correct letter for the answer.

1. Buses leave Austin for Dallas every 35 minutes. The first bus in the morning leaves at 6:10 A.M. What is the departure time closest to 11:00 A.M.?

   A 10:45 **C** 11:15
   B 10:50 **D** 11:20

2. Don needs to calculate how many 3 foot by 3 foot square tiles cover a floor that is 12 feet by 9 feet. Which strategy is used to solve this problem?

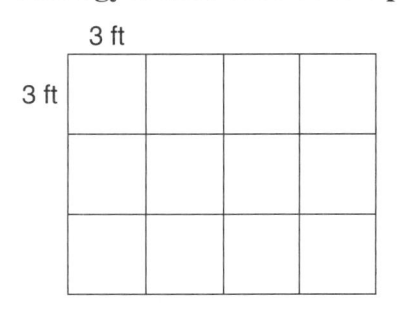

   A Make an organized list.
   B Draw a picture.
   C Write an equation.
   D Work backward.

3. Robin has 10 coins that total $0.63. If she has only dimes, nickels, and pennies, how many dimes does she have?

   A 0 **C** 5
   B 2 **D** 6

The baseball league has a concession stand. Use the price list to answer Questions 4 and 5.

Item	Price
Popcorn	$0.75
Peanuts	$0.25
Hot dogs	$1.50
Pizza	$2.00

4. Jennifer has $10.00 to spend. What is the greatest number of items she can buy if she buys an equal number of each item?

   A 4
   B 8
   C 5
   D 12

5. How much will it cost to buy 2 pizzas and 2 popcorns?

   A $2.75
   B $3.50
   C $4.00
   D $5.50

Name _____

Intervention Practice **M13**

Math Diagnosis and Intervention System

Problem-Solving Skill: Look Back and Check

Circle the correct letter for the answer.

1. You get 3 stars for each book you read. How many stars would you get if you read 5 books?

    A 3 stars
    B 5 stars
    C 10 stars
    D 15 stars

2. Ed has 2 quarters and 7 nickels in his bank. Fred has 7 dimes and 5 nickels in his bank. Ned has 9 dimes and 7 pennies in his bank. Jed has 3 quarters and 5 pennies in his bank. Who has the most money in their bank?

    A Ed   **C** Fred
    B Ned   **D** Jed

3. Bob buys a pair of jeans. The total cost is $23. He pays with a $20 bill and a $5 bill. How much change should Bob receive?

    A $25   **C** $3
    B $23   **D** $2

4. Britney has 4 apple pies. She cuts each pie into 6 pieces. How many pieces of apple pie does Britney have?

    A 24 pieces
    B 18 pieces
    C 12 pieces
    D 6 pieces

5. It costs $1 to buy a can of soda. The machine can take only quarters and nickels. How many ways can you put $1 in the soda machine?

    A 1 way   **C** 4 ways
    B 2 ways   **D** 5 ways

6. George, Mary, and Juan are fourth-graders. George is taller than Juan. Mary is shorter than Juan. Which is the correct order of students from the tallest to the shortest?

    A George, Mary, Juan
    B George, Juan, Mary
    C Mary, George, Juan
    D Juan, George, Mary

105

Name _____

Intervention Practice **M14**

Problem Solving Skill: Look Back and Check

Circle the correct letter for the answer.

1. Jason, Greg, and two of their friends went out for pizza and soft drinks. Their bill was $26.40. If they shared the cost of the pizza and soft drinks evenly, how much did each person have to pay?

   A $3.30   C $12.20
   B $6.60   D $13.20

2. Kristin traveled 1,110 miles from Atlanta to Boston. Lois traveled 2,380 miles from Los Angeles to Cleveland. How many more miles did Lois have to travel than Kristin?

   A 3,490   C 1,280
   B 2,270   D 1,270

3. Dan earns $6.00 a day in the summer doing odd jobs for his mom. If Dan works 5 days per week, how much will he earn in 8 weeks?

   A $240   C $48
   B $250   D $30

Use the data table for Questions 4–6.

| Relay Race Results ||
Runner	Time in Seconds
Amy	17.4
Keith	18.2
Patty	18.5
Max	16.8

4. If you wanted to know if the relay team won their race, which of the following would have to be calculated?

   A How many times did everyone run?
   B Who had the fastest time?
   C What was the average time?
   D How long did the four runners run in all?

5. Which is the total time for the middle school track team?

   A 35.6 seconds   C 70.9 seconds
   B 54.1 seconds   D 80.3 seconds

6. Which is the correct way to find the total time?

   A Add 17.4 and 18.2.
   B Add 17.4 + 18.2 + 18.5 + 16.8.
   C Subtract the smallest from the largest number.
   D Multiply the four numbers.

Intervention Practice **M15**

Problem-Solving Skill
Translating Words to Expressions

Circle the correct letter for the answer.

Which numerical expression matches the situation?

1. The number of tires on 3 cars when 1 car has 4 tires
   - A 3 + 1
   - B 3 × 4
   - C 3 + 4
   - D 4 − 3

2. Mr. Ramirez had 45 pencils at the beginning of the year. The class used 44 pencils.
   - A 45 + 44
   - B 44 − 45
   - C 45 − 44
   - D 45 ÷ 44

3. The total of 3 cubes, 7 spheres, and 10 cylinders
   - A 3 + 7 + 10
   - B 3 + 7 − 10
   - C 3 × 7 × 10
   - D 7 + 3 × 10

4. The cost of one ticket if all the tickets for 5 children cost $25 in all
   - A $25 − 5
   - B $5 + $25
   - C $25 × 5
   - D $25 ÷ 5

5. Harry has 30 stamps on 5 pages of his stamp album. There are the same number of stamps on each page.
   - A 5 × 30
   - B 30 − 5
   - C 30 + 5
   - D 30 ÷ 5

6. 12 boys minus 3 boys
   - A 12 − 3
   - B 3 + 3
   - C 12 ÷ 3
   - D 12 + 3

7. Twenty children were singing. Then 5 children stopped singing.
   - A 20 + 5
   - B 20 × 5
   - C 20 − 5
   - D 5 − 20

8. 4 times as tall as 8 feet
   - A 4 − 8
   - B 8 − 4
   - C 4 × 8
   - D 8 + 4

Problem-Solving Skill: Translating Words to Expressions

Circle the correct letter for the answer.

1. Which is an algebraic expression for "the product of a number and 13"?

   A $13y$
   B $13 - y$
   C $13 \div y$
   D $13 + y$

2. Which is an expression for "8 more than a number"?

   A $y \div 8$
   B $y - 8$
   C $8y$
   D $y + 8$

3. A gallon of milk contains 128 ounces. Which expression shows the number of ounces in g gallons?

   A $128 + g$
   B $128 \div g$
   C $128g$
   D $g - 128$

4. Which word phrase matches the expression $x + 8$?

   A a number increased by 8
   B 8 times a number
   C the quotient of a number and 8
   D 8 less than a number

5. Which rule will change each number in the top row to the number below it?

Number	1	2	3	4	5	6
Result	4	8	12	16	20	24

   A 3 plus the top row
   B 4 times the top row
   C 5 divided by the top row
   D 8 times the top row

6. Which of the following is a phrase for $n \div 2$?

   A a number divided by 2
   B two less than a number
   C the product of 2 and a number
   D two more than a number

7. Steven walked up 6 steps, then he walked up some more steps. Which expression shows the number of steps Steven walked up?

   A $6 \div x$
   B $6x$
   C $x - 6$
   D $6 + x$

Name _____

Intervention Practice **M17**

Problem-Solving Skill: Writing to Explain

Circle the correct letter for the answer.

1. Suppose you spin the spinner below 100 times. Which letter would you spin about the same number of times as the letter A?

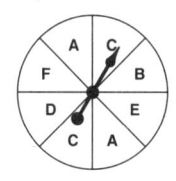

   A The letter B.
   B The letter F.
   C The letter C.
   D The letter D.

2. Su Jong has $15. Can she buy a T-shirt for $7.98 and a pair of shorts for $5.98?

   A No. The costs round to $800 and $600. $800 + $600 = $1,400, and $15 < $1,400.
   B No. The costs round to $80 and $60. $80 + $60 = $140, and $15 < $140.
   C No. The costs round to $10 and $10. $10 + $10 = $20, and $15 < $20.
   D Yes. The costs round to $8 and $6. $8 + $6 = $14, and $15 > $14.

3. Jack has 73 baseball cards and 102 basketball cards. Ron has 57 baseball cards and 296 basketball cards. Jill has 301 baseball cards and 0 basketball cards. Katie has 154 baseball cards and 51 basketball cards. Estimate who has the most cards.

   A Jack; 70 + 100 = 170
   B Ron; 60 + 300 = 360
   C Jill; 300 + 0 = 300
   D Katie; 150 + 50 = 200

4. What is the missing number?

   | Pennies saved | 1 | 2 | 3 | 4 | 5 |
   | Nickels saved | 3 | 6 | 9 | 12 | ? |

   A 6. The number of nickels is 1 more than the number of pennies.
   B 10. The number of nickels is 2 times the number of pennies.
   C 15. The number of nickels is 3 times the number of pennies.
   D 20. The number of nickels is 15 more than the number of pennies.

109

Intervention Practice **M18**

Problem-Solving Skill: Writing to Explain

Circle the correct letter for the answer.

1. You are saving your money to buy a new DVD player that costs $110. You have $35 in the bank and you deposited another $25 you received for your birthday. You received $5 a week in allowance and plan to set $2 of it aside for the DVD player. You do the following calculations and determine that it will take you 25 weeks to save enough money for the DVD player. Do any of these steps contain an error? If so, which step?

   Step 1: 35 + 25 = 60

   Step 2: 110 − 60 = 50

   Step 3: 50 ÷ 2 = 25

   Step 4: It will take 25 weeks.

   A There is an error in step 1.
   B There is an error in step 2.
   C There is an error in step 3.
   D All four steps are done correctly.

2. Angie can buy three CD's for $52.00. How much would one CD cost? Which would be the correct way to solve the problem?

   A 52 + 3
   B 52 × 3
   C 52 − 3
   D 52 ÷ 3

Use the Painting information for questions 3 and 4.

3. Ann paints houses during the summer. It takes her 7 hours to scrap off the old paint, 35 hours to paint the house, and 3 hours to clean up. She works 10 hours a day and gets paid $22 an hour. How many days does it take her to complete a house and how much does she make per house? You do the following calculations and find out Ann earns $1,210 per house and it takes her 6 days. What is the first step that contains an error?

   Step 1: 7 + 35 + 3 + 10 = 55 hours

   Step 2: 55 × $22 = $1,210

   Step 3: 55 ÷ 10 = 5.5

   Step 4: Round 5.5 to 6 days

   A There is an error in step 1.
   B There is an error in step 2.
   C There is an error in step 3.
   D There is an error in step 4.

4. Which of the following would be the correct answer?

   A $800; 5 days
   B $990; 5 days
   C $1000; 6 days
   D $1150; 6 days

Name _____

Math Diagnosis and Intervention System

Intervention Practice **M19**

Problem-Solving Skill: Writing to Compare

Circle the correct letter for each answer.

1. Use the bar graphs below. Which comparison statement is true?

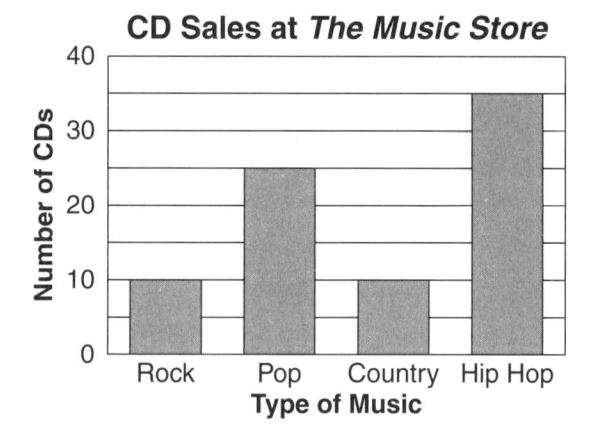

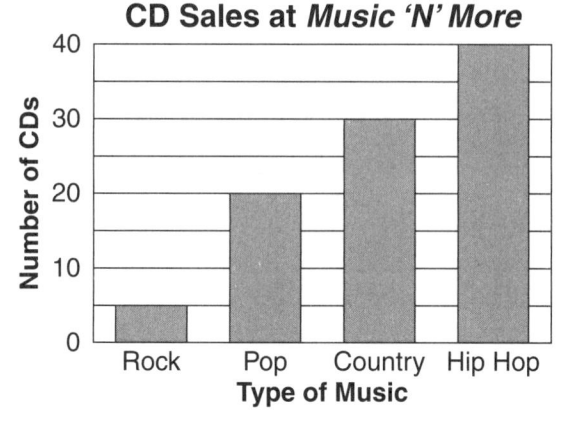

   CD Sales at *The Music Store*

   (bar graph: Rock 10, Pop 25, Country 10, Hip Hop 35)

   CD Sales at *Music 'N' More*

   (bar graph: Rock 5, Pop 20, Country 30, Hip Hop 40)

   A *The Music Store* sold the same number of country CDs as *Music 'N' More* sold.

   B *Music 'N' More* sold more pop CDs than *The Music Store* sold.

   C *The Music Store* sold fewer rock CDs than *Music 'N' More* sold.

   D Both stores sold more Hip Hop CDs than other types of CDs.

2. Betty spent $2.75 on books and $5.50 on art supplies. Jamal spent $2.90 on books and $5.25 on art supplies. Which comparison statement is true?

   A Jamal spent more on art supplies than Betty did.

   B Betty spent more in all than Jamal did.

   C Jamal spent less on books than Betty did.

   D Betty and Jamal spent the same amount in art supplies.

3. Jim, Ella, and Quan are reading the same book. So far Jim has read 72 pages, Ella has read 83 pages, and Quan has read 49 pages. Which comparison statement is true?

   A Jim has read the most pages so far.

   B Quan has read fewer pages than Ella.

   C Ella and Jim have read the same number of pages.

   D Quan has read more pages than Jim.

Intervention Practice **M20**

Problem-Solving Skill: Writing to Compare

Circle the correct letter for each answer.

Use the figures for questions 1–2.

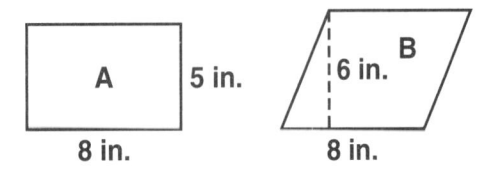

1. Which statement is true?

   A Both figures are parallelograms.

   B Figure A has 4 obtuse angles.

   C Figure B has 4 right angles.

   D Figure A has a larger area than figure B.

2. Which statement is false?

   A Figure A has a perimeter of 26 inches.

   B Figure B has an area of 48 square inches.

   C Figure B is a rhombus.

   D Figure A is a rectangle.

Use the graph for question 3.

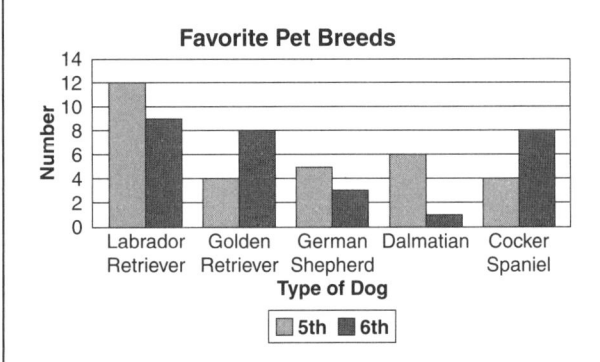

Favorite Pet Breeds

3. Mrs. Thompson's students surveyed their fifth and sixth grade classmates about the most popular dog breed. The results are shown in the graph above. Which of the four statements correctly compares the data?

   A The cocker spaniel and German Shepherd are the least popular dogs among 5th graders.

   B The most popular breed of dog between both 5th and 6th graders is the Labrador retriever.

   C The Dalmatian is more popular with 6th graders than 5th graders.

   D The Golden Retriever and German Shepherd are the least popular dog among 6th graders.

Name _____

Intervention Practice **M21**

Math Diagnosis and Intervention System

Problem Solving Strategy: Writing to Describe

Circle the correct letter for the answer.

1. Use the figures below. Which description is true?

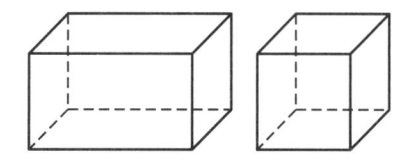

   A Both have twelve faces.
   B The rectangular prism can roll, but the cube cannot.
   C The cube has six square faces, but the rectangular prism does not.
   D Both have flat surfaces shaped like a circle.

2. Which description is true?

   A A quadrilateral has four sides, but a triangle has only three sides.
   B A rectangle and a trapezoid both have four right angles.
   C A rhombus has parallel sides, but a parallelogram does not.
   D An isosceles triangle and an equilateral triangle both have all sides the same length.

3. Which description is true?

   A Intersecting lines and parallel lines both cross at one point.
   B A right angle is greater than an acute angle but less than an obtuse angle.
   C A line segment and a ray both have two endpoints.
   D An acute angle is greater than a right angle, but an obtuse angle is less than a right angle.

4. Use the figures below. Which description is true?

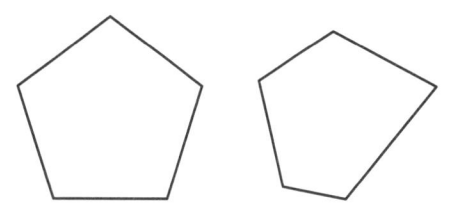

   A Both figures have 5 right angles.
   B Both figures are solid shapes.
   C Both figures have 4 sides.
   D Both figures have 5 sides.

113

Name _____

Intervention Practice **M22**

Problem-Solving Skill: Writing to Describe

Circle the correct letter for the answer.

1. Mr. Jenkins science class needs to determine how much soil they need to fill the container shown below. What is one way to find the volume of the figure shown?

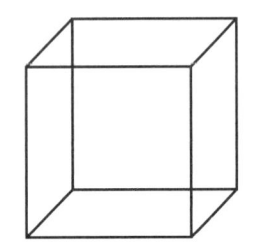

   A Find the area of the base. Add it to the height.

   B Find the area of the base. Multiply it by the height.

   C Find the area of each side. Multiply all the areas together.

   D Find the area of each side. Add all the areas together.

2. Which is the most complete description of the figure shown?

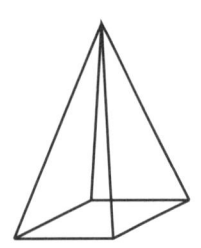

   A cube
   B polyhedron
   C rectangular prism
   D square pyramid

3. What does NOT belong in the description for the figures shown?

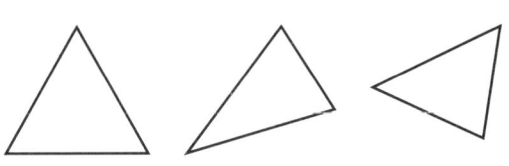

   A All are acute triangles.
   B All angles are acute.
   C All sides are different lengths.
   D All figures are polygons.

Jean took a survey to see which kind of bagel her classmates liked best. The results of the survey are shown below.

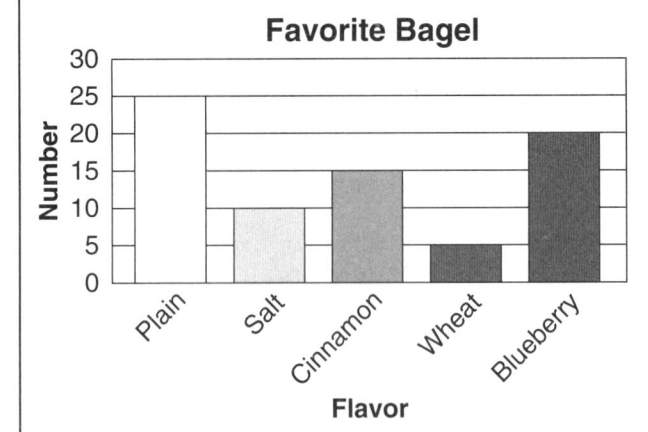

Favorite Bagel

4. Which description does not belong?

   A The bar heights are easy to read because they are multiples of 5.
   B Wheat bagels are liked by half as many students as the salt bagels.
   C Salt bagels were most popular.
   D Twice as many students liked blueberry bagels as salt bagels.

Intervention Practice **M23**

Problem-Solving Skills
Interpreting Remainders

Circle the correct letter for the answer.

1. Ashley has 75 stamps to put in a stamp album. Each page in the album holds 9 stamps. How many stamps will be on the page that is *not* completely filled?

   A 9 stamps
   B 8 stamps
   C 4 stamps
   D 3 stamps

2. The Johnson family is going to vacation in Florida. They are driving 6 hours each day. It takes 45 hours to drive to Florida. How many days will it take to drive to Florida?

   A 6 days   C 8 days
   B 7 days   D 10 days

3. Ellen had $30. She bought as many books as she could. If each book cost $7, how many books did Ellen buy?

   A 210 books
   B 30 books
   C 4 books
   D 2 books

Use the problem below for Questions 4 and 5.

Mia uses 4 yellow beads and 4 green beads to make a friendship bracelet. She has 25 yellow beads and 21 green beads.

4. How many bracelets can Mia make?

   A 8 bracelets
   B 7 bracelets
   C 5 bracelets
   D 3 bracelets

5. How many more green beads does Mia need to make one more bracelet?

   A 1 more
   B 2 more
   C 3 more
   D 4 more

6. Rashid is setting up tables for a school party. Each table seats 6 people. There will be 45 people at the party. How many tables will be needed?

   A 5 tables   C 8 tables
   B 7 tables   D 12 tables

Problem-Solving Skill
Interpreting Remainders

Circle the correct letter for the answer.

Use the information below for questions 1–2.

The decorating committee is putting 3 red carnations into each centerpiece. They have 73 red carnations.

1. How many centerpieces can they make?

   A 25   **C** 24
   B 23   **D** 20

2. How many carnations will they have left over?

   A 0   **C** 1
   B 2   **D** 3

3. During a basketball game, the Wauseon Bulldogs made 33 free throws. If 7 of the players made 4 free throws each, how many free throws did the eighth player make?

   A 5   **C** 4
   B 3   **D** 2

4. Pam has a stamp collection. The stamps are stored in albums. Each page holds 15 stamps. She has 312 stamps in her collection. How many pages will Pam use?

   A 22   **C** 21
   B 20   **D** 12

Use the information below for questions 5–6.

The Ace River Rafting Company has 62 life jackets available for people that are white-water rafting. Each raft can carry 8 people.

5. How many full rafts can Ace River Rafting supply with jackets?

   A 9   **C** 8
   B 7   **D** 6

6. How many more life jackets does Ace River need in order to supply another full raft of people?

   A none   **C** 4
   B 2   **D** 6

7. Kristin has a board that is 14 feet long. How many 4-foot sections can she cut from this board?

   A 1   **C** 2
   B 3   **D** 4

8. Each carton can hold 12 eggs. How many cartons does Tyrell need to hold 40 eggs?

   A 2   **C** 4
   B 3   **D** 5

Name _____

Intervention Practice **M25**

Math Diagnosis and Intervention System

Problem-Solving Strategy: Draw a Picture

Circle the correct letter for the answer.

1. If it takes 10 minutes to saw a log twice to make three pieces, how long would it take to cut the log into four pieces?

   A 3 minutes **C** 15 minutes
   B 13 minutes **D** 20 minutes

2. Tina is making a bracelet for her friend Sara. She puts 4 yellow beads on the chain, then 3 blue beads, then 4 yellow beads, then 3 blue beads, and so on. If she uses 16 yellow beads, then stops, how many blue beads has she used?

   A 6 **C** 12
   B 9 **D** 15

3. Four friends are waiting in line at the amusement park. Jenny is in front of Kraig. Kraig is in front of Mary. Greg is first. Who is last in line?

   A Kraig **C** Greg
   B Mary **D** Jenny

4. The parent's club is making breakfast for the teachers. The teachers have a choice of scrambled or fried eggs and home fries or potato wedges. They also have a choice of banana, cinnamon or pineapple bread. How many different breakfasts are there?

   A 12 **C** 6
   B 7 **D** 3

5. Mrs. Winston is installing lighting along her sidewalk. The length of her sidewalk is 18 feet and a light needs to be placed at the beginning and end of the sidewalk and every 2 feet. How many lights will Mrs. Winston need?

   A 8 **C** 10
   B 9 **D** 12

6. Carla gives herself 5 beads for each 2 beads she gives Anita. If Carla has 20 beads how many does Anita have?

   A 6 **C** 10
   B 8 **D** 12

Intervention Practice **M26**

Problem-Solving Strategy: Draw a Picture

Circle the correct letter for the answer.

1. You are fifth in line. Your friend is at the end of the line. There are 3 people between you and your friend. How many people are in line?

   A 6
   B 7
   C 8
   D 9

2. A rectangular photo is 10 inches high and 8 inches wide. A border around the photo is 1 inch wide. What is the perimeter of the border?

   A 44 inches
   B 3 feet
   C 20 inches
   D 40 inches

3. A necklace is made of red beads and blue beads. There are 3 red beads between every two blue beads. If there are 16 beads in the necklace, how many are red?

   A 3
   B 4
   C 9
   D 13

4. You draw 3 straight lines to divide a circle into sections. What is the most number of sections you can divide the circle into?

   A 3
   B 4
   C 7
   D 8

5. On a sign, the letter L is made up of 2 rectangles joined together. Each rectangle is 6 feet long and 2 feet wide. What is the area of the letter L?

   A 24 sq. ft.
   B 16 sq. ft.
   C 10 sq. ft.
   D 10 feet

6. Paul ran for class president and received $\frac{3}{4}$ of the votes. If he got 60 votes, how many people voted?

   A 45
   B 80
   C 100
   D 120

Name _____

Intervention Practice **M27**

Problem-Solving Strategy
Make an Organized List

Circle the correct letter for the answer.

1. A cafeteria serves 3 types of noodles with either meat or tomato sauce. How many different dinners of noodles with sauce can you make?

   A 3 **C** 9
   B 6 **D** 12

2. Matthew is going fishing. He will use worms and minnows for bait. He has 5 fishing poles. How many bait and fishing pole combinations can he use?

   A 1 **C** 10
   B 5 **D** 15

3. Your mom offers sundaes for dessert. You can choose vanilla or strawberry frozen yogurt with a topping of nuts, coconut, fruit, or chocolate sauce. If you can have one flavor of yogurt and one topping, how many choices do you have for a sundae?

   A 4 **C** 8
   B 6 **D** 10

4. A candle-making kit contains 5 scents and 4 colors of wax. How many combinations of candles can you create using one color and one scent?

   A 4 **C** 9
   B 5 **D** 20

5. Sofia's Café offers a brunch special of eggs and your choice of bacon, sausage links, or sausage patties. You can order your eggs scrambled, fried, or poached. How many different combinations of the brunch special are possible?

   A 9 **C** 15
   B 12 **D** 18

6. Maria needs to do her chores. She has to make her bed, water the plants, sweep the kitchen, and dust the living room. In how many different orders can she do her chores?

   A 8 **C** 24
   B 12 **D** 48

119

Name _____

Intervention Practice **M28**

Problem-Solving Strategy: Make an Organized List

Circle the correct letter for the answer.

1. Three people are in line. In how many different orders can they stand?

    A 3
    B 4
    C 5
    D 6

2. How many 4-digit odd numbers can you make using the digits 2, 3, 4, and 6? You may use each digit only once.

    A 6
    B 9
    C 12
    D 24

3. You have 3 letter tiles: L, W, and O. You use all three to try to make a word. What fraction of the possible arrangements spell a real word?

    A $\frac{1}{6}$
    B $\frac{1}{3}$
    C $\frac{3}{6}$
    D $\frac{6}{2}$

4. A *BigTime* meal has a sandwich and a drink. There are 3 types of sandwiches and 3 types of drinks. How many different *BigTime* meals are there?

    A 3
    B 6
    C 9
    D 12

5. Five children are playing in a chess tournament. How many games are needed for each child to play every other child one time?

    A 20
    B 16
    C 10
    D 6

6. How many 2-digit numbers can you make from the digits 1, 3, 5, 7, and 9 if you use each digit once?

    A 5
    B 6
    C 8
    D 20

© Pearson Education, Inc.

120

Name _____

Intervention Practice **M29**

Problem-Solving Strategy: Make a Table

Circle the correct letter for the answer.

1. Jacob and Mark each began biking today. If Jacob bikes 4 miles each day and Mark bikes 6 miles each day, how many miles will Jacob have biked when Mark has biked 30 miles?

   A 16 miles   **C** 24 miles
   B 20 miles   **D** 28 miles

2. Nicholas needs to place 6 cups on each table for the picnic. If there are 8 tables, how many cups will he need?

   A 14   **C** 52
   B 48   **D** 58

3. Lee made the same number of birdhouses each day. Which number will complete the table for the number of birdhouses Lee has completed during 4 days?

Day	1	2	3	4
Birdhouses	7	14	21	?

   A 42   **C** 36
   B 32   **D** 28

4. Lydia recorded the height of a sunflower. The first week, the plant was 3 inches high. The second, third, and fourth week, it was 5 inches, 7 inches, and 9 inches high. At this rate, when will the sunflower be 15 inches high?

   A 5 weeks   **C** 6 weeks
   B 7 weeks   **D** 8 weeks

5. Jenna bakes cookies every third day. Her best friend Wanda bakes cookies every fourth day. If they both baked cookies today, in how many days will they both be baking cookies again?

   A 7 days   **C** 9 days
   B 12 days   **D** 15 days

6. Max needs to water each of his pepper plants with 2 cups of water. How many cups of water will he need for 5 pepper plants?

   A 7 cups
   B 10 cups
   C 12 cups
   D 14 cups

Intervention Practice **M30**

Problem Solving Strategy: Make a Table

Circle the correct letter for the answer.

1. A leaky faucet drips 3.0 mL of water in 20 seconds. At that rate, how much water will drip in 3 minutes?

   A   23 mL
   B   27 mL
   C   36 mL
   D   60 mL

2. You have $73.50. If you spend $11.50 each week, in how many weeks will you have less than $10.00

   A   1
   B   2
   C   4
   D   6

3. In a group of children, there are 5 boys for every 6 girls. How many boys are there in the group if there are 48 girls?

   A   30
   B   40
   C   50
   D   60

4. Each pound of snack mix uses 2 ounces of peanuts, 5 ounces of raisins, and some other ingredients. A batch of mix has 12 ounces of peanuts. How many ounces of raisins does it have?

   A   30 oz.
   B   24 oz.
   C   22 oz.
   D   19 oz.

5. It takes you from 1:45 P.M. to 2:15 P.M. to walk 1.5 miles. If you keep walking at that rate, how far will you have walked by 3:15 P.M.?

   A   3.0 miles
   B   3.5 miles
   C   4.5 miles
   D   6.0 miles

6. You have 5 pounds of cat food. If your cat eats 7 ounces each day, when will your supply fall below 2 pounds? [1 pound = 16 ounces]

   A   in 5 days
   B   in 6 days
   C   in 7 days
   D   in 12 days

Name _____

Intervention Practice **M31**

Problem-Solving Skill: Make a Graph

Circle the correct letter for the answer.

Use the graph for Questions 1–3.

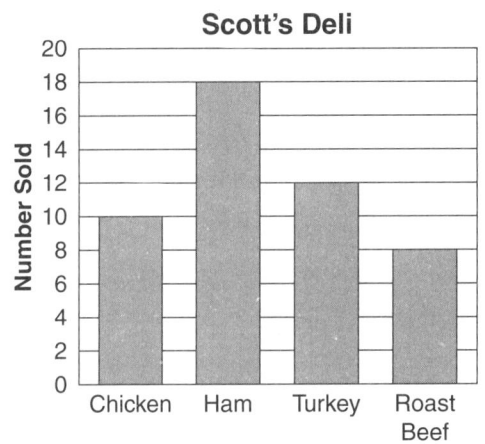

Scott's Deli

(bar graph: Chicken 10, Ham 18, Turkey 12, Roast Beef 8; y-axis: Number Sold; x-axis: Type of Sandwich)

1. How many chicken sandwiches were sold?

   A 8 C 10
   B 12 D 18

2. How many more turkey sandwiches were sold than roast beef?

   A 12 C 8
   B 6 D 4

3. How many more of the most popular sandwich were sold than the least popular?

   A 18 C 12
   B 10 D 8

Use the graph for Questions 4–6.

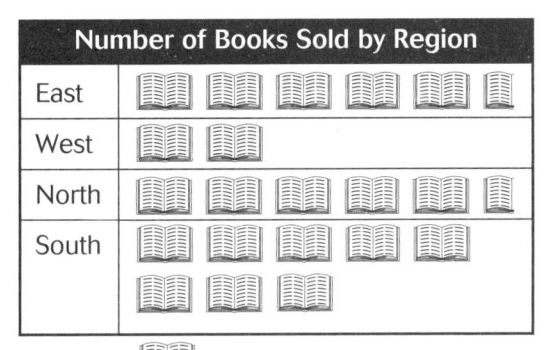

Number of Books Sold by Region
East: 6 books
West: 2 books
North: 6 books
South: 9 books

Key: Each 📖 represents 10 books each.

4. Which region sold the most books?

   A East C West
   B North D South

5. How many books were sold in the West?

   A 2 C 10
   B 20 D 30

6. How many more books were sold in the South than the North?

   A 80 C 55
   B 25 D 20

7. How many total books were sold?

   A 220 C 210
   B 200 D 21

123

Name _____

Intervention Practice **M32**

Problem-Solving Strategy: Make a Graph

Circle the correct letter for the answer.

Make a graph with the data in the table to answer Questions 1–3.

Gina's Finances		
Year	Income	Expenses
1999	$1,000	$900
2000	$800	$600
2001	$600	$700
2002	$900	$900

1. In what year did Gina's income equal her expenses?

   A 1999
   B 2000
   C 2001
   D 2002

2. In what year were Gina's expenses larger than her income?

   A 1999
   B 2000
   C 2001
   D 2002

3. In what year did Gina have the most difference between her income and expenses?

   A 1999
   B 2000
   C 2001
   D 2002

4. Use the graph to answer Questions 4–5. What does this graph show?

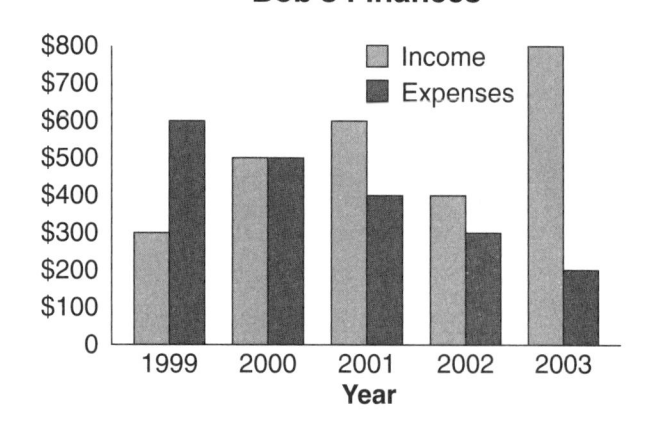

   Bob's Finances

   (Bar graph showing Income and Expenses for years 1999–2003)

   A Bob's income gets smaller every year.
   B Bob's income is always larger than his expenses.
   C Bob's expenses were the largest in 2002.
   D Bob's expenses get smaller each year.

5. In what year was Bob's expenses the same as his income?

   A 1999
   B 2000
   C 2001
   D 2002

Intervention Practice **M33**

Problem Solving Strategy: Use Objects

Circle the correct letter for the answer.

1. You have 2 copies of a photo of a dog and 4 copies of a photo of a cat. In how many different ways can you arrange them with one photo on each side of a cube?

   A 2
   B 3
   C 4
   D 6

2. You make a square by trimming one side of an $8\frac{1}{2} \times 11$ inch sheet of paper. Which estimate is closest to the actual area of the square?

   A 120 sq. in.
   B 110 sq. in.
   C 70 sq. in.
   D 20 sq. in.

3. Which pattern can be folded to form a cube?

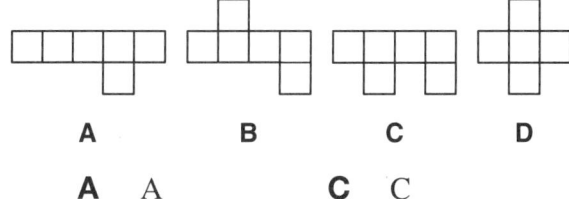

   A   B   C   D

   A A
   B B
   C C
   D D

4. A cube has 8 vertices. If you cut one corner with a single cut, how many vertices will the cube have?

   A 12
   B 10
   C 8
   D 6

5. You are putting beads on small rings. Each ring has 3 green beads and 2 yellow beads. If each green bead must touch at least one other green bead, in how many different orders can you arrange the 5 beads?

   A 1
   B 2
   C 3
   D 4

125

Math Diagnosis and Intervention System

Intervention Practice **M34**

Name _____

Problem-Solving Strategy: Act It Out

Circle the correct letter for the answer.

1. Tori wants to buy a bag of pretzels from a vending machine that cost $0.70. If she has one quarter and the rest are dimes and nickels in her wallet, what are the least number of coins she can pay with?

   A 3   **C** 4
   B 5   **D** 6

2. Brenda has 13 animal crackers. Vince has 3 animal crackers. Brenda wants Vince to have the same number of animal crackers that she has. How many should she give him?

   A 3   **C** 4
   B 5   **D** 6

3. Judy has a square sheet of paper. How many times should she fold it to get 8 triangles that are all the same size?

   A 3
   B 5
   C 4
   D 6

4. What are the least number of straws you would need to make 6 congruent triangles? (Hint: 1 straw can form a side of two different triangles.)

   A 12   **C** 16
   B 18   **D** 24

5. Maggie and Seth look for fossils on a beach. In the morning they find 11 fossils. In the afternoon they find 6 more. Their father has 5 more for them. If they want to share the fossils, how many should each child get?

   A 4   **C** 6
   B 11   **D** 22

6. There are 21 children waiting in line to be admitted into a roller-skating rink. Olivia is seventh in line. How many more children are there behind her than in front of her?

   A 6   **C** 8
   B 7   **D** 14

Name _____

Intervention Practice **M35**

Problem-Solving Strategy: Look for a Pattern

Circle the correct letter for the answer.

1. What is the next figure in the pattern?

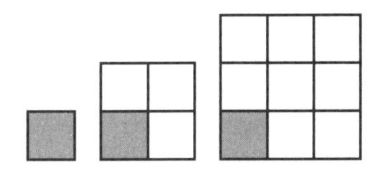

   A 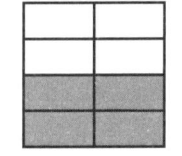   C

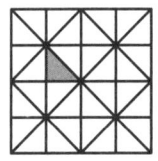

   B 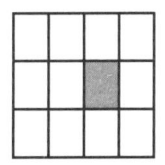   D

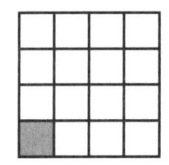

2. What is the next number in the pattern?

   9, 12, 15, 18, 21, 24, …

   A 25   C 27
   B 29   D 32

3. Hobby's is having a grand opening and giving out prizes. The prizes will be given out according to a pattern. The store will give a prize to the 8th, 16th, 24th, and 30th customer who enters the store. Which customer will get the next prize?

   A 32nd   C 38th
   B 36th   D 40th

4. What is the pattern?

   40, 36, 32, 28, 24, 20

   A add 4
   B subtract 4
   C add 2 and subtract 1
   D subtract 6

5. Each house on Tony's street has an odd number. If the first house is 211, what is the fourth house?

   A 213   C 215
   B 217   D 219

6. Which number would complete the pattern?

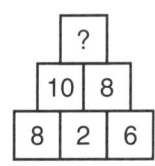

   A 20   C 18
   B 10   D 6

7. What is the next number in the pattern?

   $$50 + 5 = 55$$
   $$505 + 50 = 555$$
   $$5{,}005 + 500 = 5{,}505$$

   A 50,005 + 5,000
   B 50,500 + 500
   C 50,000 + 500
   D 55,055 + 5,050

127

Intervention Practice M36

Problem-Solving Strategy: Look for a Pattern

Circle the correct letter for the answer.

1. What is the next number in the pattern?

    2187, 729, 243, 81, ?

    A 8
    B 9
    C 27
    D 36

2. Which figure comes next in the pattern?

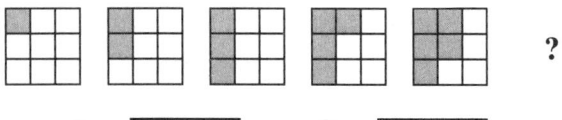

    A 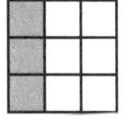
    B 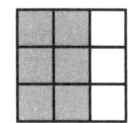
    C 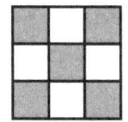
    D

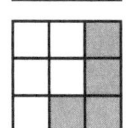

3. Which time comes next in the pattern?

    8:40, 9:30, 10:20, ?

    A 11:00
    B 11:10
    C 11:20
    D 11:30

4. How many blocks are needed to make the seventh bridge in this pattern?

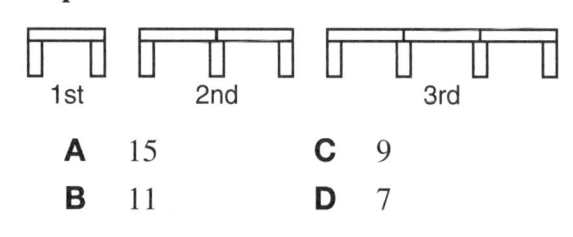

    1st   2nd   3rd

    A 15
    B 11
    C 9
    D 7

5. The rectangular tablecloth has a repeating pattern. How many squares on the whole tablecloth are gray?

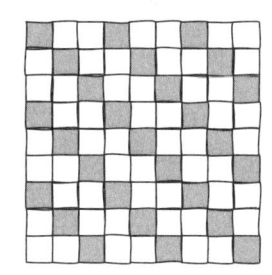

    A 58
    B 48
    C 36
    D 27

6. What are the next numbers in the pattern?

    $2\overline{)8}=4$, $2\overline{)9}=4R1$, $2\overline{)10}=5$, $2\overline{)11}=5R1$,

    A $2\overline{)14}=7$
    B $2\overline{)12}=6$
    C $2\overline{)13}=6R1$
    D $6\overline{)12}=2$

128

Name _____

Intervention Practice **M37**

Problem-Solving Skill: Try, Test, and Revise

Circle the correct letter for the answer.

1. Raul bought 1 football card and 1 baseball card. The football card cost twice as much as the baseball card. Raul spent $12. What was the cost of the baseball card?
   - A $2
   - B $6
   - C $4
   - D $8

2. Lisa has 15 bunnies in all. She has 3 more brown bunnies than gray bunnies. How many gray bunnies does she have?
   - A 3
   - B 9
   - C 6
   - D 11

3. Tony delivers pizza. In his money pouch are 8 bills worth $28. If he only has $1 and $5 bills, how many $5 bills does he have?
   - A 2
   - B 4
   - C 3
   - D 5

4. 2 adults and 3 children ride the bumper cars for $14. If the adult's fare is twice as much as the child's fare, what is the adult fare?
   - A $1
   - B $3
   - C $2
   - D $4

Use the information in the table for Questions 5–6.

Taylor Groceries	
Eggs	$1
Peanut Butter	$4
Sausage	$3
Cherry Pie	$6
Cheese	$2

5. Mollie bought 2 different items. She spent $8. Which items did she buy?
   - A peanut butter and sausage
   - B cherry pie and sausage
   - C cheese and cherry pie
   - D eggs and cherry pie

6. Christopher bought 3 different items and spent $9. Which items did he buy?
   - A peanut butter, sausage, and cheese
   - B cherry pie and sausage
   - C eggs, peanut butter, and cheese
   - D sausage, peanut butter, and eggs

7. Sally and her dad have a combined height of 108 inches. Sally is half the height of her dad. How tall is Sally?
   - A 72 inches
   - B 54 inches
   - C 40 inches
   - D 36 inches

129

Intervention Practice **M38**

Problem Solving Strategy: Try, Test, and Revise

Circle the correct letter for the answer.

1. The quotient of two numbers is 4 and the sum is 90. If you try the numbers 60 and 30, the sum will be exactly right and the quotient will be

   A   too low
   B   too high
   C   exactly right
   D   can't tell

2. A rectangle has a perimeter of 26 cm. The length is 7 cm greater than the width. If you try a length of 12 cm, the perimeter you calculate will be

   A   too low
   B   too high
   C   exactly right
   D   can't tell

3. The area of a rectangular rug is 24 square yards and its perimeter is 22 yards. What are the dimensions of the rug?

   A   12 yd by 2 yd
   B   9 yd by 2 yd
   C   6 yd by 4 yd
   D   3 yd by 8 yd

4. How can you separate these five numbers into two groups so that the sum of the numbers in each group is the same?

   16, 13, 9, 17, 5

   A   5, 9, 13 and 16, 17
   B   5, 9, 17 and 13, 16
   C   5, 9, 16 and 13, 17
   D   can't be done

5. Fourteen people each bought a drink. They spent a total of $27.50. How many of them bought a large drink?

   DRINKS
   Small $1.75 each
   Large $2.50 each

   A   12
   B   10
   C   8
   D   4

Intervention Practice **M39**

Problem-Solving Strategy
Write a Number Sentence

Circle the correct letter for each answer.

1. Hazel is 52 inches tall. Her brother Francis is 37 inches tall. How many inches taller is Hazel than Francis?
   - **A** 5
   - **B** 15
   - **C** 25
   - **D** 89

2. One aquarium at the zoo has 9 fire salamanders and 3 tegu lizards. How many animals are in that aquarium?
   - **A** 3
   - **B** 16
   - **C** 12
   - **D** 27

3. A passenger van can seat 12 passengers. If 36 flute players need to be driven to a band concert, how many vans will be needed?
   - **A** 432
   - **B** 24
   - **C** 3
   - **D** 2

4. Muffins from Unlimited Bakery are packaged 6 in a box. John purchases 5 boxes for a meeting at work. How many muffins did he buy?
   - **A** 1
   - **B** 11
   - **C** 30
   - **D** 40

5. There are 8 players on Kasandra's soccer team and 2 more than that on Michael's team. How many players are on Michael's team?
   - **A** 4
   - **B** 10
   - **C** 16
   - **D** 18

6. On Tuesday the high temperature reached 78 degrees. On Wednesday the high temperature was 84 degrees. How many degrees warmer was Wednesday's high temperature?
   - **A** 16
   - **B** 12
   - **C** 8
   - **D** 6

7. Jennifer's mother cut 15 pieces of watermelon for a family picnic. At the end of the picnic, 7 pieces were left. How many pieces of watermelon had the family eaten?
   - **A** 8
   - **B** 9
   - **C** 12
   - **D** 22

Intervention Practice **M40**

Problem Solving Strategy: Write an Equation

Circle the correct letter for the answer.

1. You pay $63.43 for a video game. That includes a tax of $3.48. How much does the video game cost before tax? Which word equation best fits the problem?

   A cost before tax + tax = cost after tax

   B cost before tax − tax = cost after tax

   C cost before tax × tax = cost after tax

   D cost before tax ÷ tax = cost after tax

2. The perimeter of a rectangular park is 840 yards. The park is 170 yards wide. How long is the park? If l stands for the length of the park, which equation best fits the problem?

   A $840 - l = 170$

   B $2l + 340 = 840$

   C $l + 340 = 840$

   D $l \div 170 = 840$

3. Two sides of a triangular banner are 14 inches long and 18 inches long. The perimeter is 48 inches. How many inches long is the other side of the banner?

   A 36 inches

   B 32 inches

   C 20 inches

   D 16 inches

4. Ryan can type 40 words per minute. At that rate, how long would it take him to type 1000 words?

   A 2 hours, 50 minutes

   B 1,040 minutes

   C 25 minutes

   D 5 minutes

Intervention Practice   M41

Problem-Solving Skill: Use Logical Reasoning

Circle the correct letter for the answer.

1. Jerry is playing hide-and-seek with his little sister. She could hide in the bedroom, playroom, living room, kitchen, or bathroom. Use the clues below to find out what room she hid in.
   The room did not have a sink.
   People do not sleep here.
   There are no toys found in this room.

   A   living room
   B   kitchen
   C   playroom
   D   bedroom

2. Tina, Joe, Pam, Michelle, and Nan are in a race. Tina finishes first. Pam finishes before Nan and after Michelle. Joe finishes last. In what order did they finish the race?

   A   Tina, Michelle, Nan, Pam, Joe
   B   Tina, Nan, Michelle, Pam, Joe
   C   Tina, Michelle, Pam, Nan, Joe
   D   Tina, Pam, Michelle, Nan, Joe

3. Micah, Ric, Julio, and Cal are playing soccer. They have maroon, red, jade, and clear water bottles. Use the clues to determine what color water bottle Julio had.
   The color of Cal's water bottle began with the same letter as his name. The other boys did not. Ric's water bottle was hard to find because it blended in with the grass.

   A   maroon   C   red
   B   jade   D   clear

4. Simon is thinking of a number between 45 and 55. There is no 4 in the tens place. It is not divisible by 2. The sum of its digits is not 6.

   A   50   C   53
   B   51   D   54

5. The secret number is an odd number between 30 and 40. The sum of its digits is 10. What is the number?

   A   46   C   33
   B   38   D   37

133

Intervention Practice **M42**

Problem-Solving Strategy: Use Logical Reasoning

Circle the correct letter for the answer.

1. Gloria, Helen, and Isabel have the different middle names listed. None of them have middle names with the same number of letters as their first name. What does that tell you?
   Julie, Mina, Paula

   A Gloria's middle name is Julie.
   B Isabel's middle name is Paula.
   C Helen's middle name is Mina.
   D Gloria and Isabel have the same middle name.

2. Ms. Arvada, Mr. Benson, and Ms. Chan ride different vehicles: a car, a motorcycle, and a truck. Together, Mr. Benson's vehicle and Ms. Chan's vehicle have 6 wheels. Together, Ms. Arvada's vehicle and Ms. Chan's vehicle also have 6 wheels. Who rides the motorcycle?

   A Ms. Arvada   C Ms. Chan
   B Mr. Benson   D can't tell

3. Bob, Fran, Kito, and Lynn each like different types of music. Kito plays in the orchestra. Bob likes music from the 1970s. Fran plays a saxophone in a band. What music does Lynn like?

   A classical   C rock
   B jazz   D rap

4. Romania, Sudan, Thailand, Uruguay are in four different continents. Uruguay's continent does not start with a vowel. More than half of the letters in Romania's continent and Thailand's continent are vowels. Which continent is Sudan in?

   A Africa
   B Asia
   C Europe
   D South America

5. Mary Anderson, the Biro Brothers, Earle Dickson, and Frank Henry Fleer invented bubble gum, the windshield wiper, the Band-Aid™, and the ballpoint pen. Fleer's invention is the tastiest. Dickson's is sticky, and Anderson's is used on cars. What did the Biro Brothers invent?

   A Band-Aid
   B bubble gum
   C ballpoint pen
   D windshield wiper

Intervention Practice **M43**

Problem-Solving Skill: Solve a Simpler Problem

Circle the correct letter for the answer.

1. The Marker family is putting a fence around their garden to keep the rabbits out. The garden is square. If there will be 15 posts on each side of the garden, how many posts will they need altogether?

    A 64   **C** 54
    B 56   **D** 50

2. How many diagonals can be drawn in the figure shown?

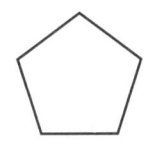

    A 5   **C** 14
    B 9   **D** 20

3. The cross-country ski trails at Oak Openings have signs posted every 300 yards. There is also a sign to mark the start of each trail. Alice starts on the red trail and has just passed the fourth sign. How far has she skied on the red trail?

    A 300 yards   **C** 1,500 yards
    B 900 yards   **D** 1,800 yards

4. Sammy and his friend Don are organizing the Boy Scout knot-tying contest. They have a piece of long rope that they need to cut into 20 pieces. How many cuts must they make?

    A 20   **C** 15
    B 19   **D** 10

5. Ryan numbered the note cards for his report, 1 through 25. How many digits did he write?

    A 10   **C** 39
    B 25   **D** 50

6. For an art project, Beth needs to cut strips of paper 4 inches long and 1 inch wide from a sheet of paper that is 8 inches long and 6 inches wide. How many strips can she cut?

    A 2   **C** 12
    B 10   **D** 48

Intervention Practice **M44**

Problem-Solving Strategy: Solve a Simpler Problem

Circle the correct letter for the answer.

1. Which of the choices has the same answer as the problem in the box?

   $$38.42 \times 3.07 \div 38.42$$

   A $(38.42 \times 38.42) \times 3.07$
   B $38 \times 3 \div 38$
   C $(38.42 \div 38.42) \times 3.07$
   D $38.42 \div 3.07 \div 38.42$

2. What is the area of the shaded figure?

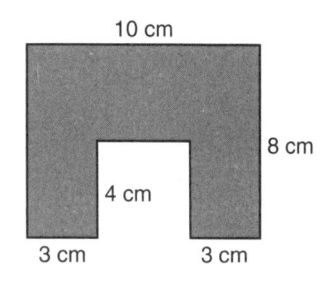

   A 80 cm^2
   B 72 cm^2
   C 64 cm^2
   D can't tell

3. What is the area of the shaded figure?

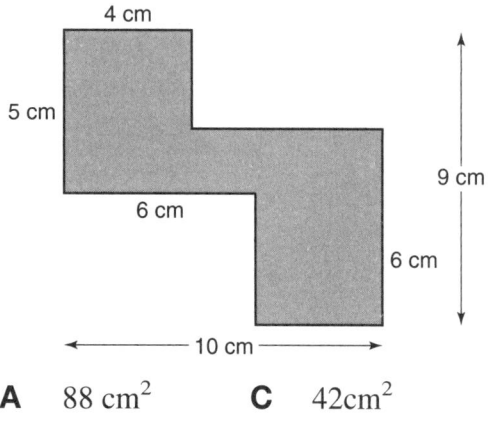

   A 88 cm^2 C 42cm^2
   B 48 cm^2 D can't tell

4. You are making a cube with 5 red faces and 1 green face. How many different cubes are possible?

   A 1
   B 2
   C 5
   D 6

5. How many rectangles are in a row of 6 squares? Remember, a square is a rectangle.

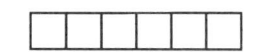

   A 21
   B 18
   C 15
   D 6

Name _____

Intervention Practice **M45**

Problem-Solving Strategy: Work Backward

Circle the correct letter for the answer.

1. On the way home from school, Thomas lost 5 marbles, then he gave 3 to Max. When he got home, he had 6 marbles. How many marbles did he have when he left school?

   A 16   **C** 12
   B 14   **D** 8

2. Tina needs to arrive at school at 7:35 A.M. It takes her 10 minutes to walk to school and 45 minutes to get ready in the morning. What is the latest time she can get up in the morning so that she arrives at school on time?

   A 7:00   **C** 6:40
   B 6:45   **D** 6:25

3. A box has red and blue marbles. You put in 4 red marbles. You take out 1 blue marble. There are 8 marbles at the end, and the probability of selecting blue was $\frac{3}{8}$. How many red marbles were in the box at the start?

   A 0   **C** 2
   B 1   **D** 3

4. At the Craft Barn, you purchased a set of acrylic paints for $6 and 2 identical paintbrushes. You spent a total of $14. What was the cost of 1 paintbrush?

   A $8   **C** $5
   B $6   **D** $4

5. Jim divides a bag of candy into 5 equal piles. He gives 4 of the piles to friends and keeps one for himself. He eats 7 pieces of candy and has 5 pieces remaining. How many pieces of candy were in the whole bag?

   A 60   **C** 36
   B 48   **D** 24

6. Lee takes 15 minutes to shower and dress, 10 minutes to eat breakfast, and 20 minutes to do his chores and walk to his bus stop. If the school bus picks him up at 7:40 A.M., what is the latest time Lee can get up in the morning?

   A 6:45   **C** 6:55
   B 6:50   **D** 7:00

Intervention Practice **M46**

Problem-Solving Strategy: Work Backward

Circle the correct letter for the answer.

1. To get from the school to the firehouse, you go 4 blocks East, turn left, and go 2 blocks North. Which directions will take you from the firehouse to the school?

   A Go 2 blocks North, turn right, and go 4 blocks West.

   B Go 4 blocks South, turn right, and go 2 blocks West.

   C Go 2 blocks South, turn right, and go 4 blocks West.

   D Go 2 blocks South, turn left, and go 4 blocks.

2. After 5 is added to a mystery number n, the sum is multiplied by 4. Then 18 is subtracted. The result is 30. Which equation can be solved to find the mystery number?

   A $30 - 18 \times 4 = n + 4$
   B $(n + 5) \times 4 - 18 = 30$
   C $n \times 4 + 5 = 30$
   D $n - 5 \div 4 + 18 = 30$

3. A store owner reduced the price of a television by $50. Then he cut the price in half. The final sale price was $120. What was the original price?

   A $10   **C** $190
   B $110   **D** $290

4. If you multiply a number by 5, then subtract 10, and then divide by 3, you get 5. What is the number?

   A 5   **C** 15
   B 10   **D** 45

5. You divide a number by 4, then add 2, and then multiply by 6. What is the number?

   A 12
   B 24
   C 100
   D not enough information

6. Marty must catch the bus at 7:10 A.M. It usually takes him 15 minutes to walk to the bus stop. He stops to eat for 20 minutes. What time must he leave home to be on time for the bus?

   A 7:05 A.M.   **C** 6:40 A.M.
   B 6:50 A.M.   **D** 6:35 A.M.